THE CIELONAUT

lost
in a poetry of stars

FRANK PREM

Publication Details

Title: *The Cielonaut*
ISBN: 978-1-925963-55-7 (p-bk)
ISBN: 978-1-925963-59-5 (e-bk)

Published by Wild Arancini Press 2024

A catalogue record for this book is available from the National Library of Australia

Cover Image source: NASA Image and Video Library (https://images.nasa.gov/)

I lose myself among these too bright lights.

Contents

About The Cielonaut *1*

The Cielonaut *5*

Image Sources *179*

Author Information *183*

Other Publications *187*

What Readers Say *191*

Index of Poems *197*

About *The Cielonaut*

The Cielonaut is sole survivor of an accident on lift off. His interstellar ship is on a journey across the universe, with no direction, and under no control. The weight of dead companions travels with him as a personal burden.

The life he has left behind is gone. Lost among the vagaries of lightspeed and light-time. The future is an unknown emptiness.

This poetry collection is an exploration of mood and emotion in a lost soul, with the awe of stars and galaxies only adding to the profound loneliness of *The Cielonaut.*

Images used in *The Cielonaut* have been taken from the *NASA Image and Video Library (https://images.nasa.gov/)*. References are given for each image.

The author extends a heartfelt thank you to NASA for making this wonderful resource accessible for general use, and for this collection of poetry. Also, for allowing the author to wallow in his own sense of awe at the wonder that is our universe.

The Cielonaut

(prelude): astro-bear

I will place
a bear
with you

a soft-furred
teddy bear

a smiling face
to keep you company
while you travel

I could wish you
a golden bower bird

a cup of rain

perhaps
a tree
from the forest

the mountain ash
from beside
the track you always walked
when you were younger

with your dog

but these are things
that belong to the earth
that belong
to where they are

so
take this little yellow bear
to place beside
the panel
of your instruments

or keep it
maybe
on the bunk
where you will lay down
for your times of rest

take it
anyway
as a piece
of me

on your journey
to the stars

when you look at it
you might see
my eyes

when you look at it
you might see
me

I will not
be waiting
I
will go to dust
but
the memory

of who

of what I am to you

will beat
as a heart
in this
sentimental
astro-bear

and I will live
in a small-bear way
for you

... ... beacon, I follow ...

light the beacon

hold the light

shine the way

oh
my love
I will follow

... ... I come ...

here I come

bring me
through
the darkness

here I come

now
I
am the shooting star

it is me
into the universe

here
I come

… … shine …

these are
the stars
you know

this
is space

where nothing
twinkles
but . . .

it shines

… … what she will see …

the night
will come

the night
will see

.

.

.

I am here
with nothing
to hide

let her
cast her eyes

yes
cast them
where she will

let the night come
let her see

this

is who I am

a little lost

he counts
as a year goes by

measures the time
in heartbeats

sixty pulses
to every minute

now
how many lightyears
have just gone dark
behind him

same again
in one minute more

and still
the emptiness
shows no sign
of an end

still
there is no chance
that anyone
will find him

that anyone
at all
is seeking

he thinks back
recalls
one year

a thousand light moments
ago

that he knew
has been dead
forever
in just one year

except himself

sole survivor
of a tragic
lift off

sole
cabin crew

sole lonely captain
of an uncontrolled
tin can
to the cosmos

it doesn't feel
as though he is moving fast
it is more
like standing still

but the gradual
rearrangement of stars
outside the porthole
reminds him
again

of exactly
where he is

... ... eternity waiting ...

she waits
the slow return

she will wait
forever

she was
once
but now
is not

she is only
an idea
of

then

still waiting

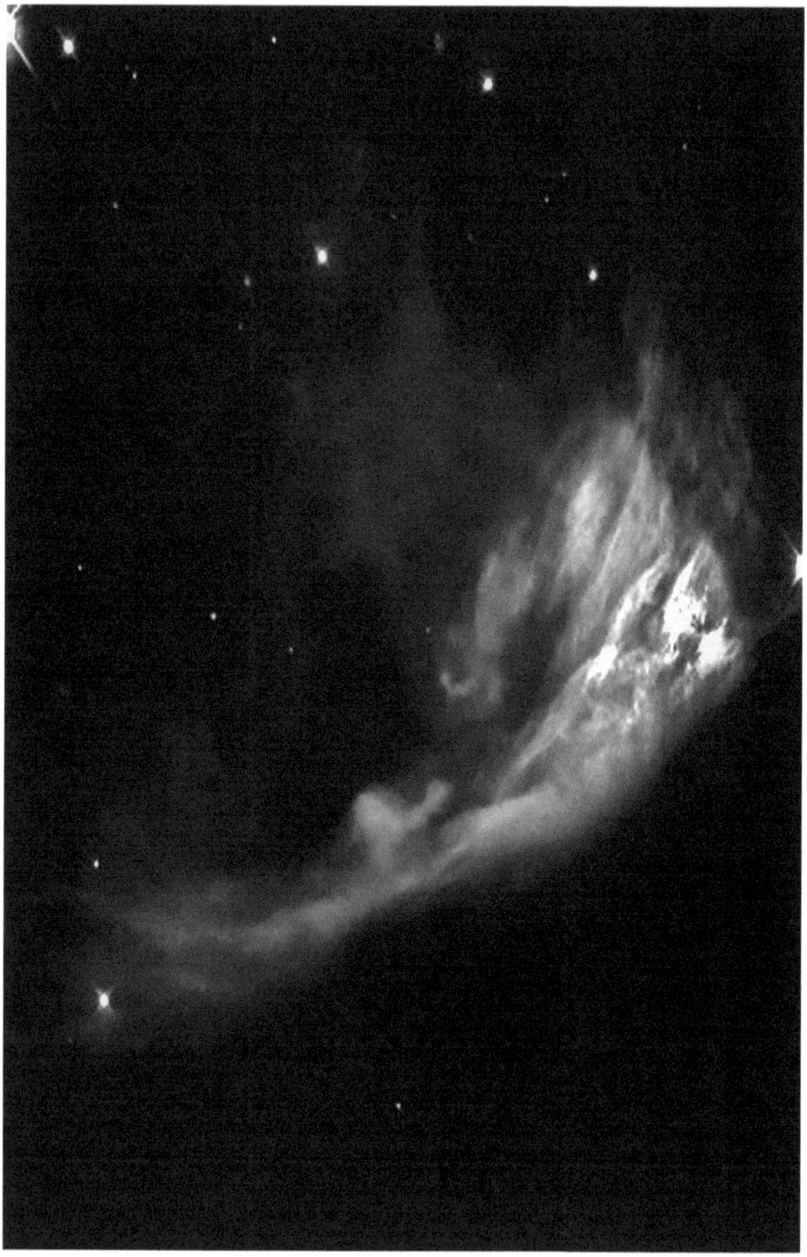

... ... good night ...

tuck the blanket
to your chin

snuggle down

it's time
for sleeping

here come your dreams

the shepherd star
will sing you
a lullaby

lull-a-bye

good
night

… … by the veil …

by veil
I see where she has been

by veil
I will follow

a path of sequins
through the dark

the milk-white trail
into
a starry
tomorrow

... ... for orion ...

a red wind blows
from orion's belt

it crosses stars
to find me

it brings the heat
from orion's heart

in wind
and in flame

a star-fire mane

I cannot look
but
I go there

blindly

data to the distance

he pens the poetry
of deep space
entered via keyboard
at a console

all his memories
from a long lost
once upon . . .

he creates them
in flowing collections
of sweet verse

each set laid out
exactly
seven poems long

then encrypted
as a string of ellipses
that will follow their leader
like a line
of hopeful ducklings
when he transmits
a data package

a single package
every one hundred
and sixty-eight
shipboard hours

aimed at a place
that might as well be
a thousand years ago

home
somewhen
away in a lost distance

... ... ochre ...

I have drawn
a man
in red and black

I have drawn him
on my wall

the ochre
of the stars
has become his skin

and he is speaking
I believe
to someone

he is speaking
I believe
to a higher place

to a
dimension
that is beyond me

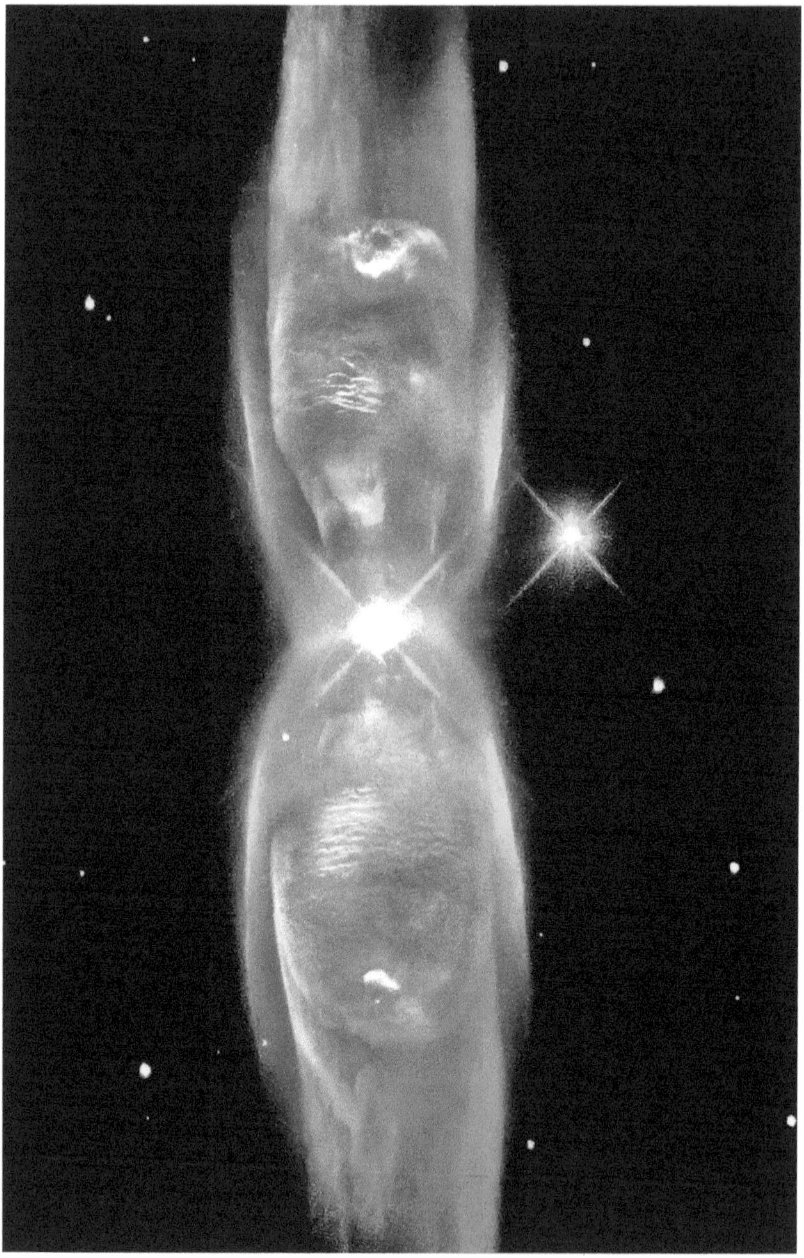

… … swim …

there is a
place
in this deep
dark
ocean

a place
for me to swim
alone

here
in the wide

in the black

here
where the lights
are spangled suggestions
of . . .

something . . .

somewhere

this
is the place
in the deep
dark
ocean
the place I swim
alone

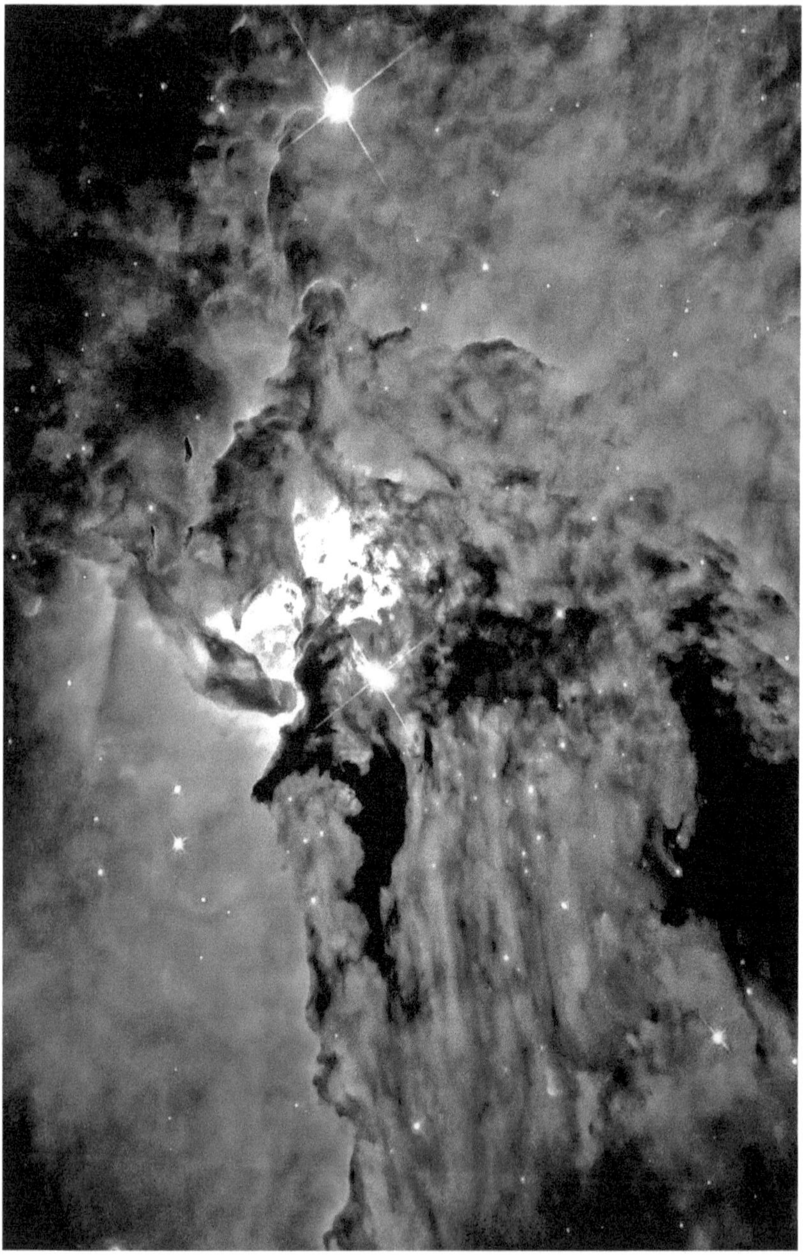

… … drop and run …

from the palette
of my colours
I will paint the night

paint
a star-scape

~

one drop
dark

and one colour
run

one fusion

a speck
for every heart

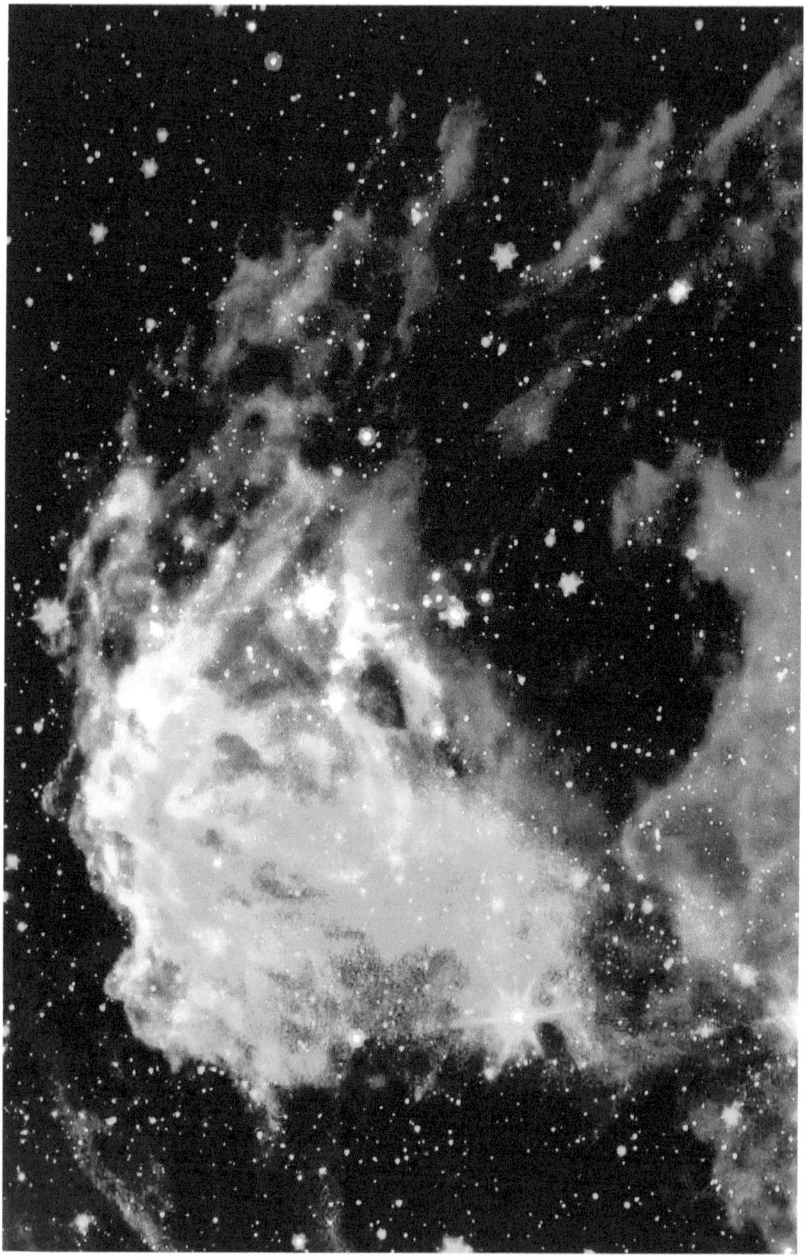

... ... *young stars* ...

young stars
at play

they surge
and they soar
around every by-way
in heaven

let the stuff
of mighty matter
roar

young stars
won't heed

they have no attention
to spare

these young stars
young
rainbow stars
play

and play

until they fill
all of the spaces

the vast emptiness
of heaven

in prison for the term of no when

who could have foreseen
a prison

back in the days
when dreams
were a welcome
expression
of desire

this ship
is not small
but he knows it
in intimate centimetres

he has walked the floors
conversed
with intelligent corners
then returned

unerringly

to here
where the leash
is tightest

the control room

the *no-control* room
says it truer
but
he can watch
be reassured
the ship
is flying

even as time passes
and he greys
gradually

with the creep of age

he can be reassured
that his ship
is flying

to *no where*

to *no when*

to no one

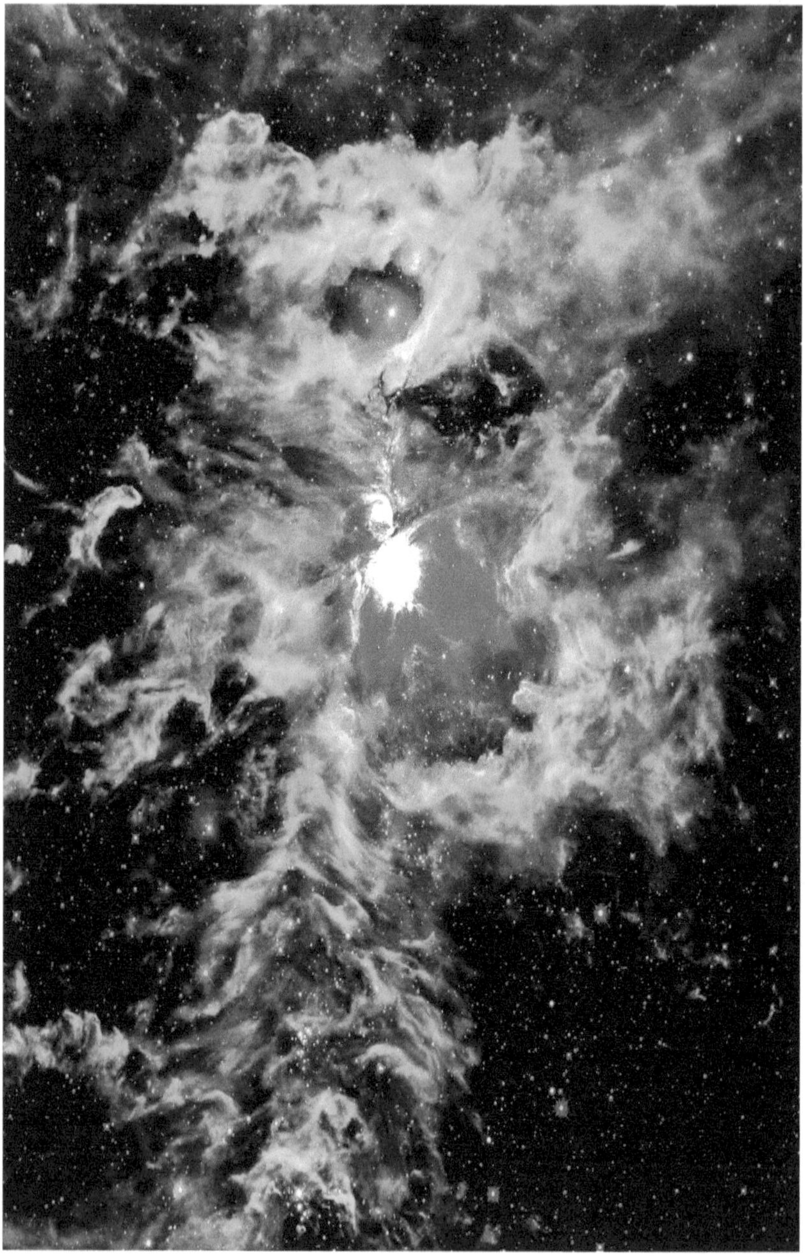

… … flows green my heart …

these
flowing mountains
run

ink

greening
away from the beat
of my heart

… … dance with the scorpion …

I dance
to the touch
of the scorpion's claw

I leap
like a wraith
of the night

the star light
is free
and the darkness is wide

so I dance
in the claw
tonight

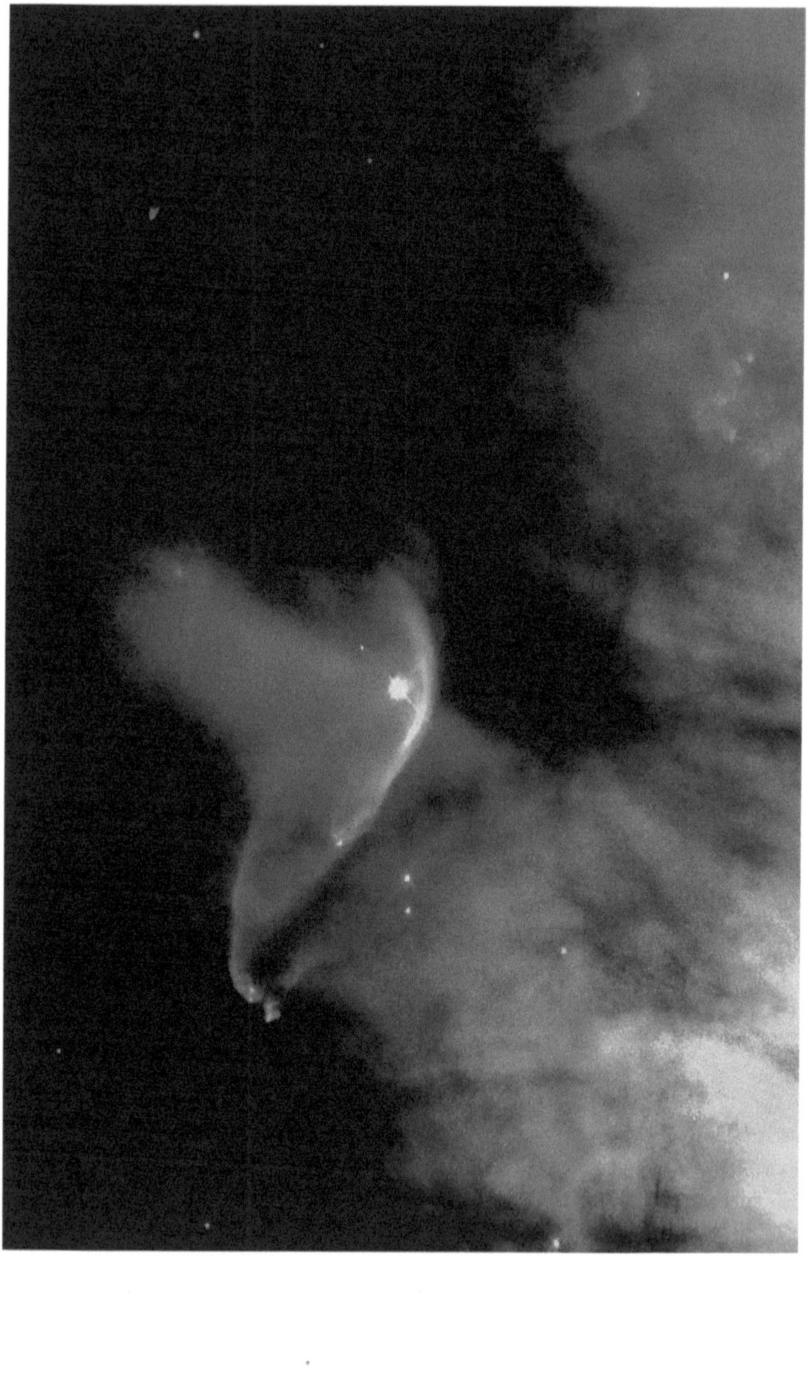

... ... *search for blue* ...

face in a mask

skirting across
a sea
of rainbow shades

of green

what is your intention

where
do you go

are you searching
for a bauble
lost

a planet
blue

I too
will seek

beside you

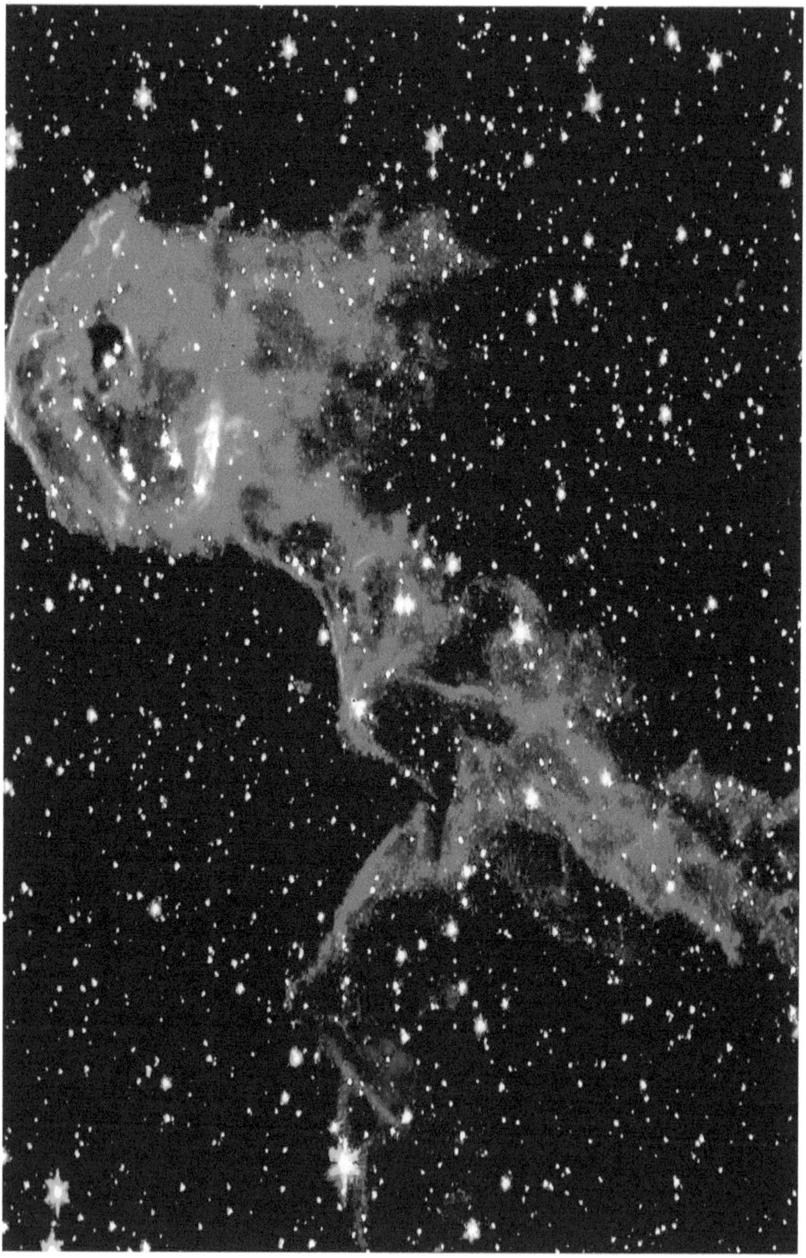

… … go by …

go

run like the wind

there is never an end

so just
go

there is none
but the sky

none

only me

pass me again
by
and by

gravity

in the viewing hall
there is no
spin

it is only himself
that is turning
in slow rotations
around
the windowed room

no light
but starlight
no weight
at all

nothing
but the vast
and the sense
that *he*
is nothing

a speck
unseen
crossing a pointless universe

unnoticed

his face is struck
from time to time
by raindrops

salty
raindrops

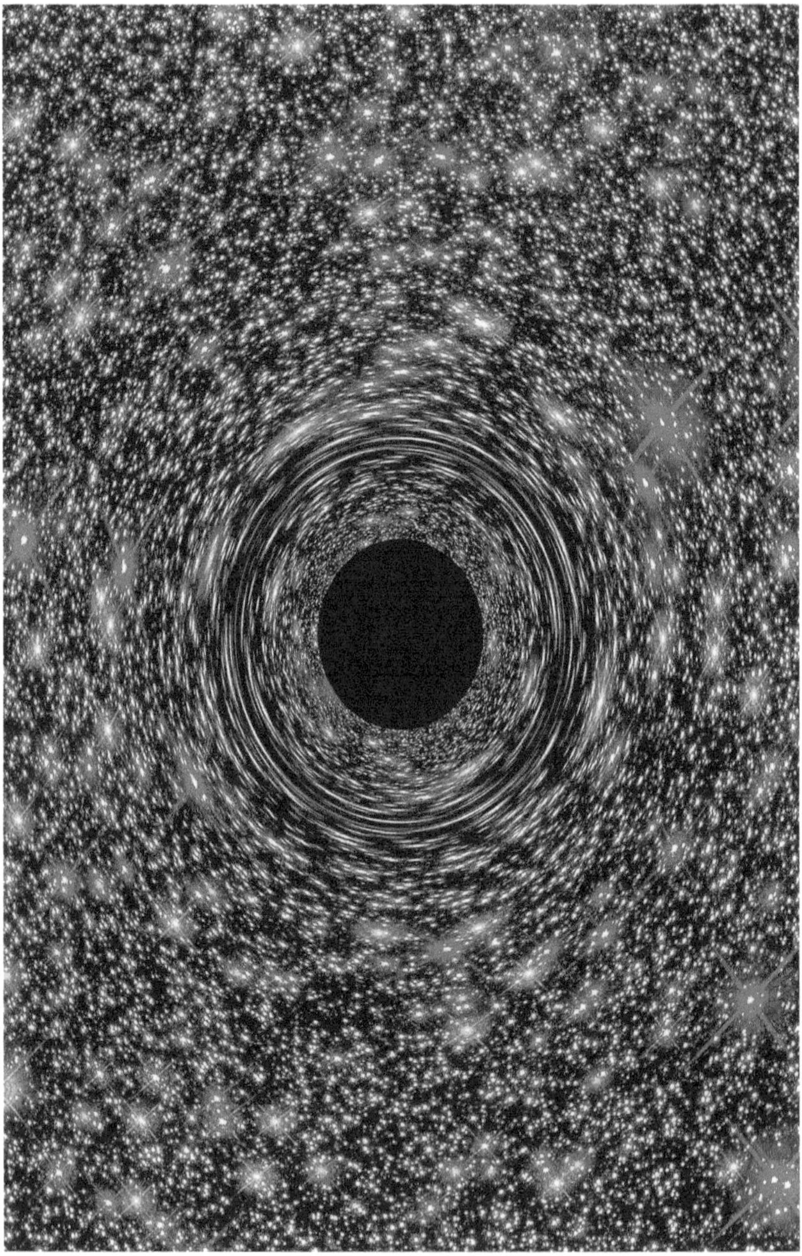

… … *one more turn (around)* …

should I
turn around
again

will I fall . . .

onto my face

I can feel myself
beginning
to giddy

I don't know
where
I left my feet
maybe I am walking
on air

but
one more time
around . . .

I will be
gone

I think that
I
will be
gone

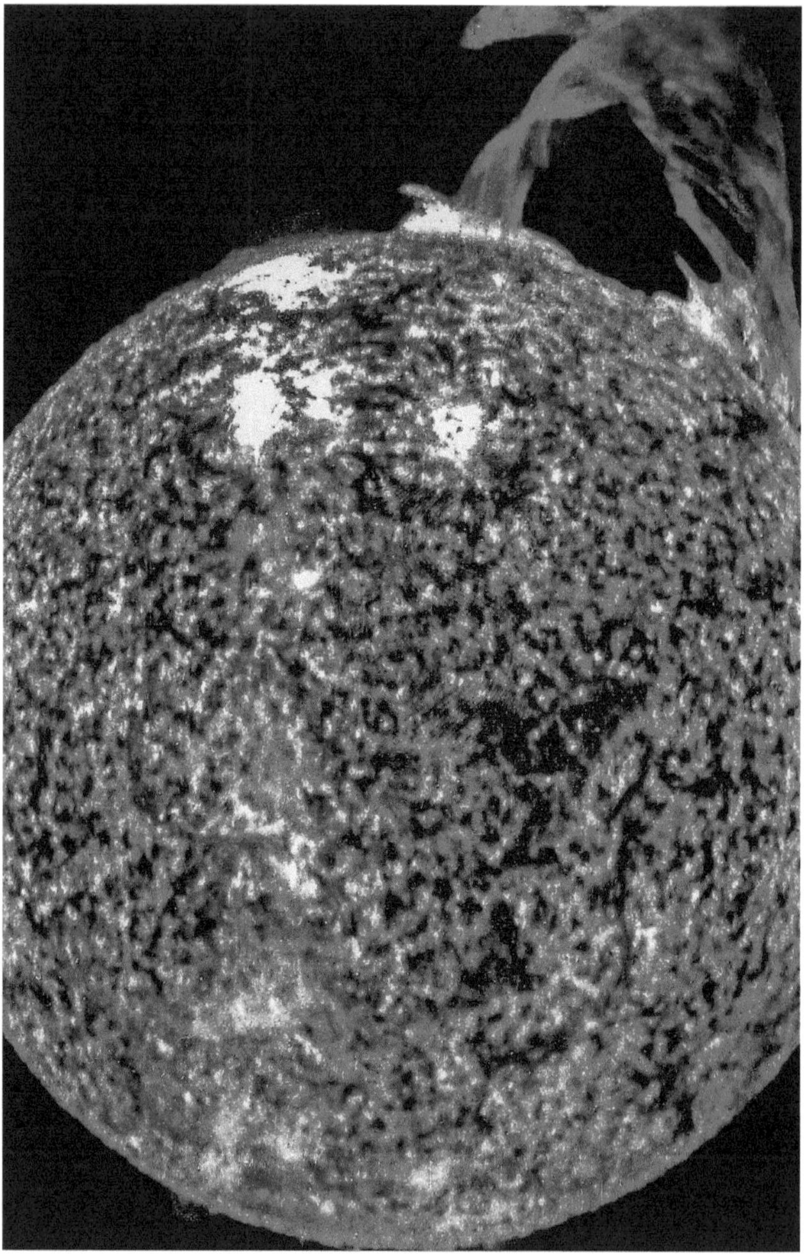

… … from you to me …

and I will fly away
one day

leave you

the sun
behind me

loop
around darkness
that I never see
because . . .

you

yes

I will fly away

leave all that you are
behind me

leap into the un-
known

beyond you

and the sun
everything

I ever was

to find
me

… … first …

is the topaz
or . . .

is it
the umber

where I
am bound

.
.
.

is it a star
some way away
in the further light

the further dark

.
.
.

topaz first
and then

beyond

… … oh heart …

oh
heart of mine

oh heart
of mine

your will
the beat

your will
the time

bang the drum
for freedom

bang that drum
for mine

let me find
my peace
at last

heart

oh
heart
so fine

ever named ever written

his mother . . .

his sister . . .

the nurse
at the *cielo-centre*
who showed him
so much . . .

such selflessness

.
.
.

the people he met –
comrades –
through his training days
striving hard
to achieve
all that was needed
to make this journey

his father
who always pointed his head
and eyes
upward –
beyond the destruction
and fragility
of the earth –
and out
among the stars

his young love
the first love
and the smile she wore
that he can still

bring to mind

and the symbolism
of a furry
yellow
teddy bear
now supervising this
nothing-life
from a seat
on a console

remembered
and remembered

he writes them

writes their names

in semidarkness
he gazes out
through a porthole
at vast emptiness

turns back
and keys their names

... ... what else ...

there
goes my heart

there
is the place

doesn't matter
the what or the why
my aim
is straight

and
true

yes
it is true
so
here I go

I
trailing
ever after

... ... *eye of the night* ...

is there life
out there

am I
completely alone

tell me
what you see

... ... a laugh around ...

heart
like a wheel

I turn
around
and around

heart like a wheel
I spin

emotions
turn
around and around

I weep
when I pause
to think

I laugh

and go around
and around

… … eagle care …

eagle
flies the wide sea

eagle wings
through
the wide sea

to catch a lonely fish
who swims
unaware

catch your fish

splash me

oh eagle
do you care

the sound

silence
is not an absence
of sound

silence is a noise

a static
pushing through the background
nothing

filling it up
completely
with the sensation
of its absence

sometimes
he finds himself
engaging the audio
of the ship

the capacity
of the ship
to listen

and plays the sound
inside
his chosen listening place

the radio
of the universe

the *nothing*
that is the static
of *everything*

... ... on ...

who will be
my home

where will be
the one
I rest with

I kiss the air
you breathe

journey on

journey on

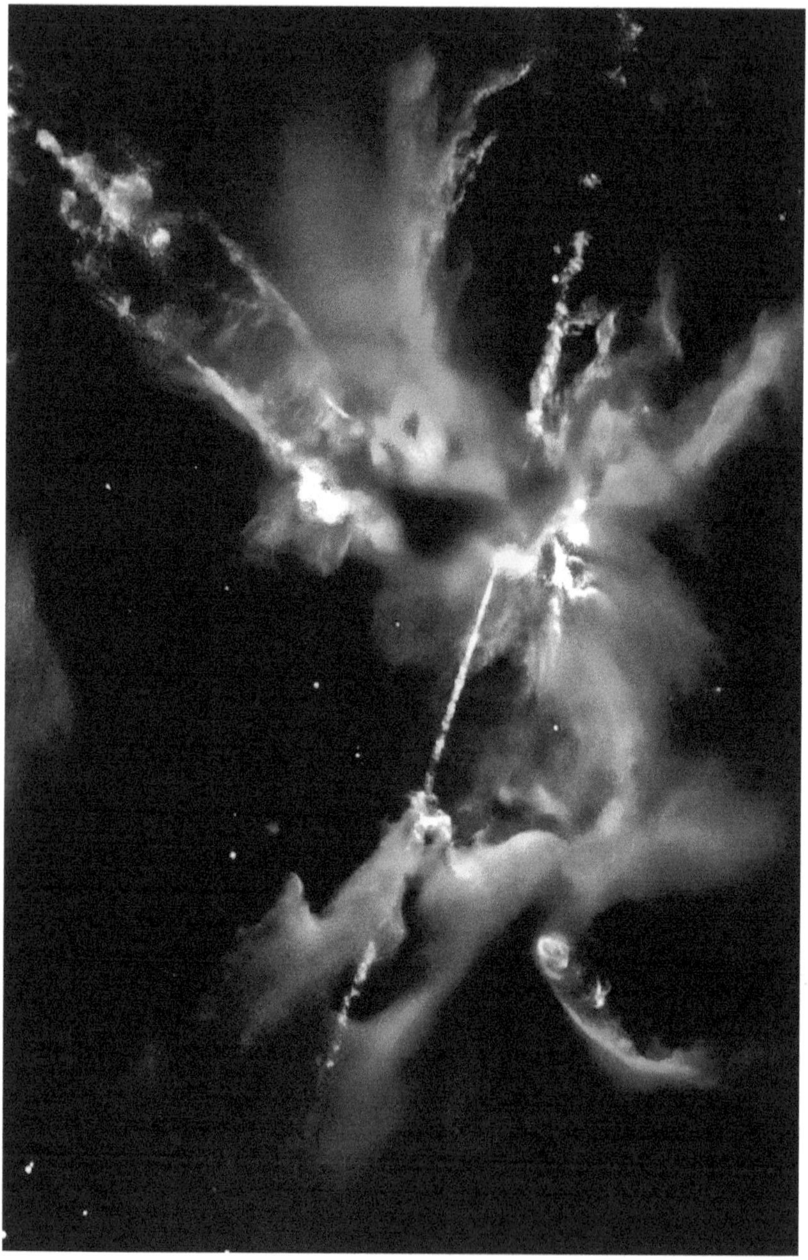

… … already claimed …

the lightning rod
of god
in my path

a smiting . . .

an anger
in heaven

let the hand
that holds the spear
smite me

here
I am

I have no fear

already I
have been wholly
claimed

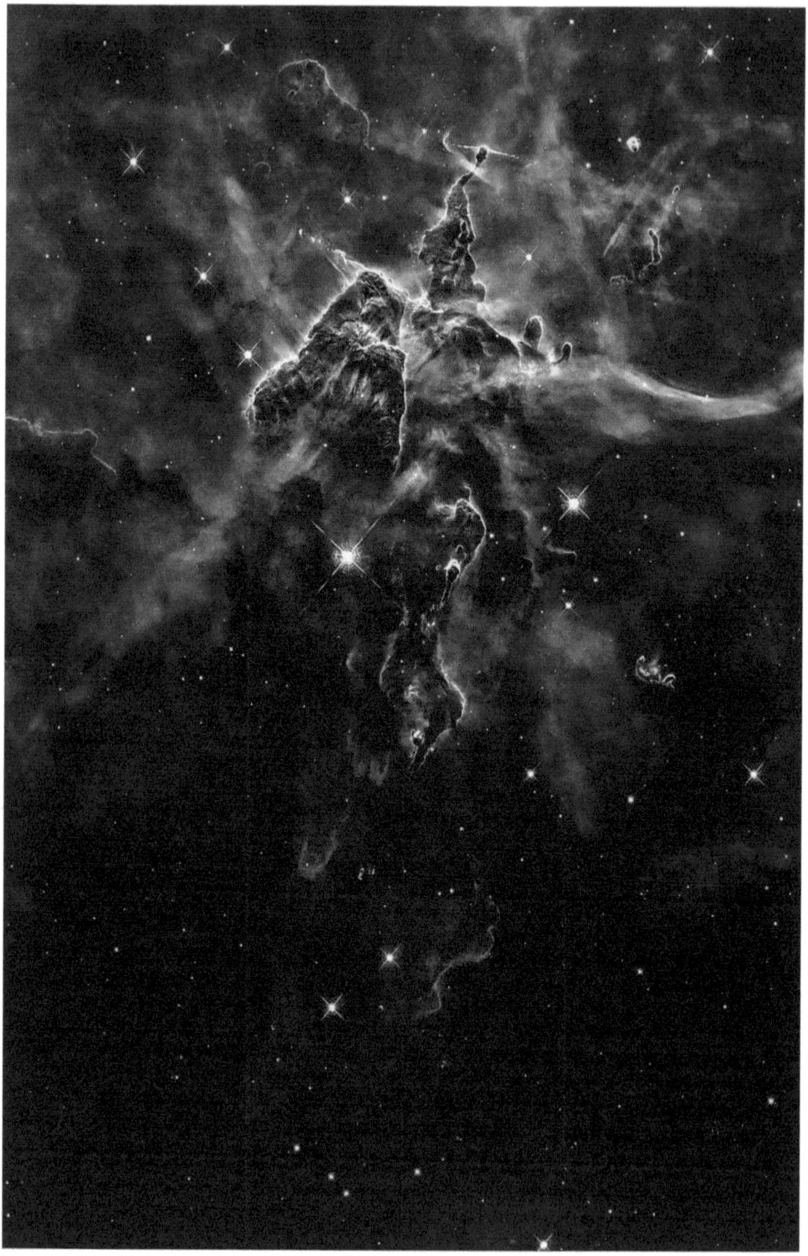

... ... what might ...

should I
adopt the posture
that is
a giant stance

cause myself to become
much bigger

should I
hunch my shoulders
martial-art
my fists and arms

can I punch
above my weight
and through the matter
that is empty space
around me

what good
is force –
wield it as I might –
when it is used against
so much
nothing

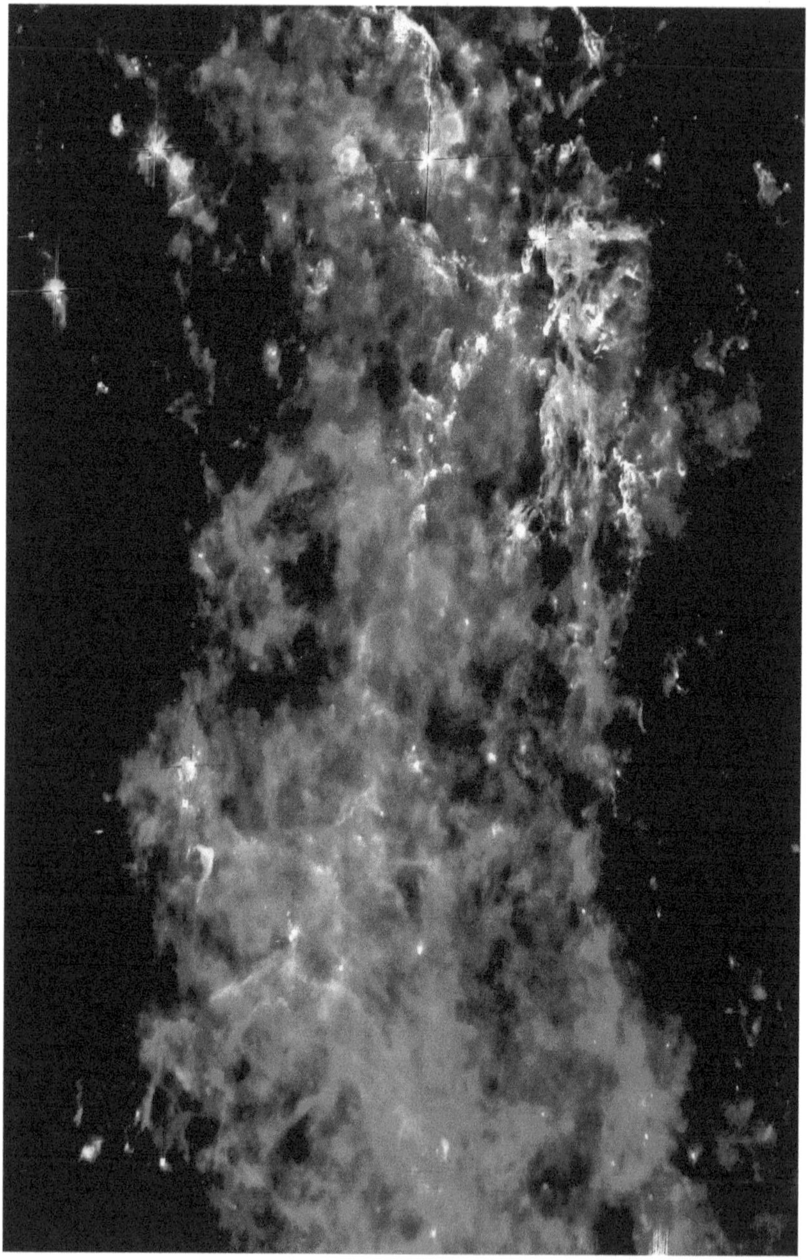

… … sing (a birthday song) …

as though a gift
unwrapped
for the birthday
of the world

of a world

a somewhere

I will sing
for you
a birthday song
from
the core
of me

just give me
a moment

just
one
small moment
to find a voice

then
I will sing

to catch a star

he toys
with his body wastes

one week
he stores them up for release
as a sudden jettison
of what has passed
through him

out
into the vastness

he is able to peer
through the porthole
as he presses a button
to watch the dispersal
of his days

a gradual drift
that becomes distance . . .

away

poo
multiplied to the power
of light speeds

at other times
in
other weeks
dump-and-release
is the order
of proceedings

not wanting to think
about the waste pollution
he personally is adding
to the cosmos

not wanting
to remember
the slow
slow
departure
of his colleagues

the *would-be*
now-jettisoned
colleagues

who have commenced
an altogether more intimate
voyage
to catch a star

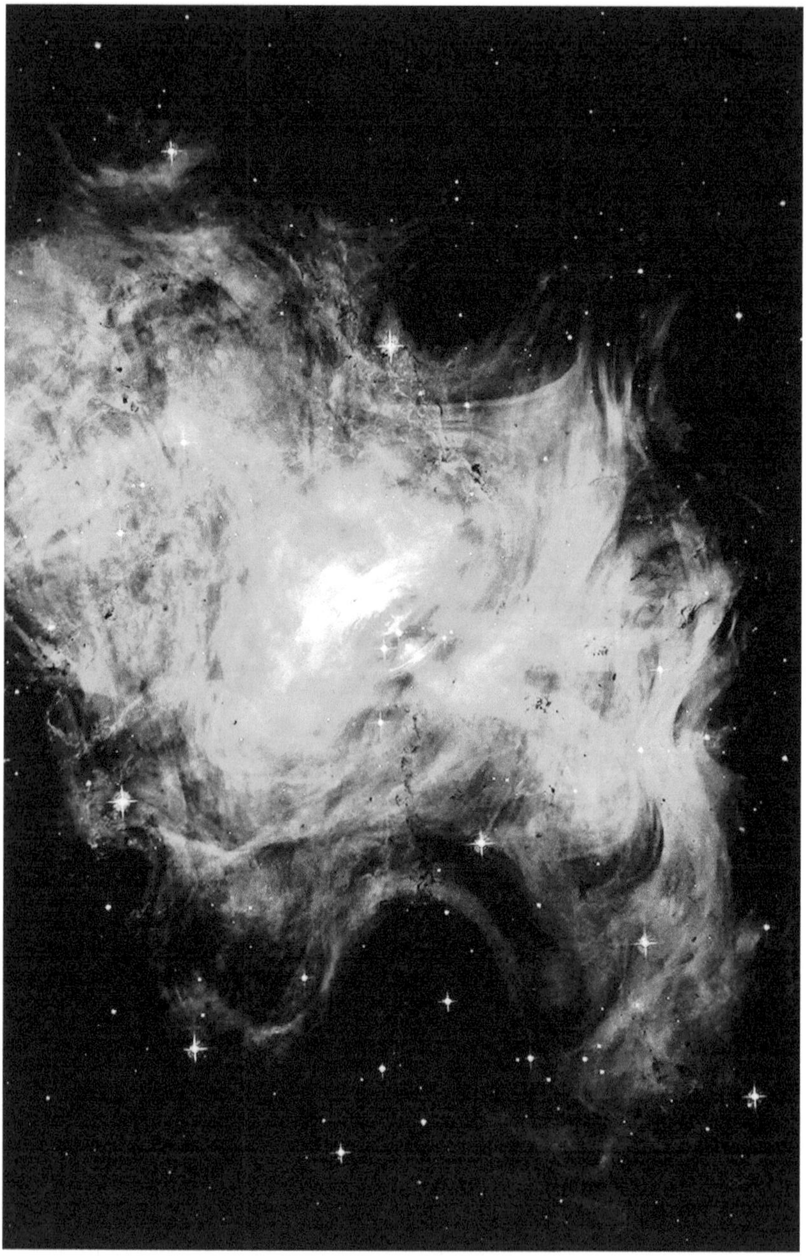

... ... rock the table ...

is there
someone
out there . . .

is someone
trying
to speak . . .

rock the table

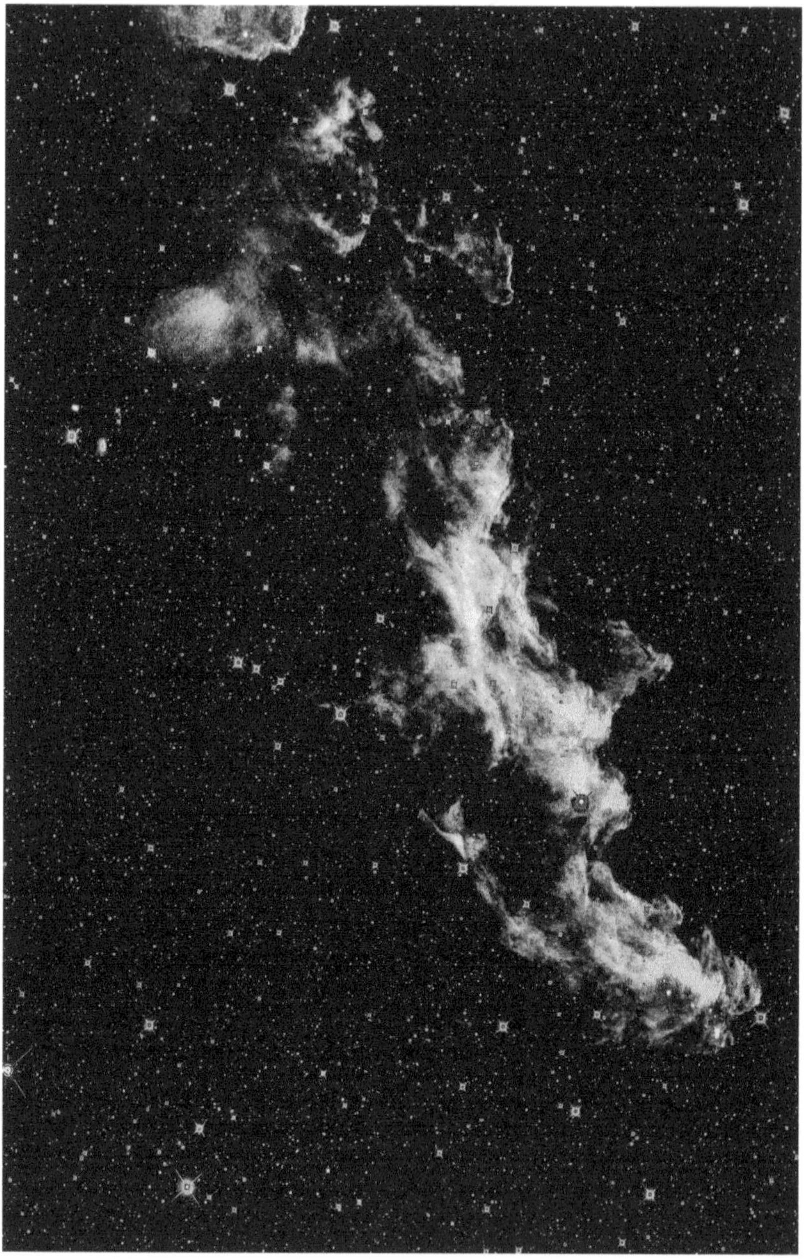

… … my love sees …

the gaze
is
into the cauldron

this time
far away
among stars

but add a drop
of contemplation
(stirring)

add
a drop of thought

(stirring)

(stirring)

my love
is the way head

my love
is the storm
I fly right into

my love
is the path

I travel home

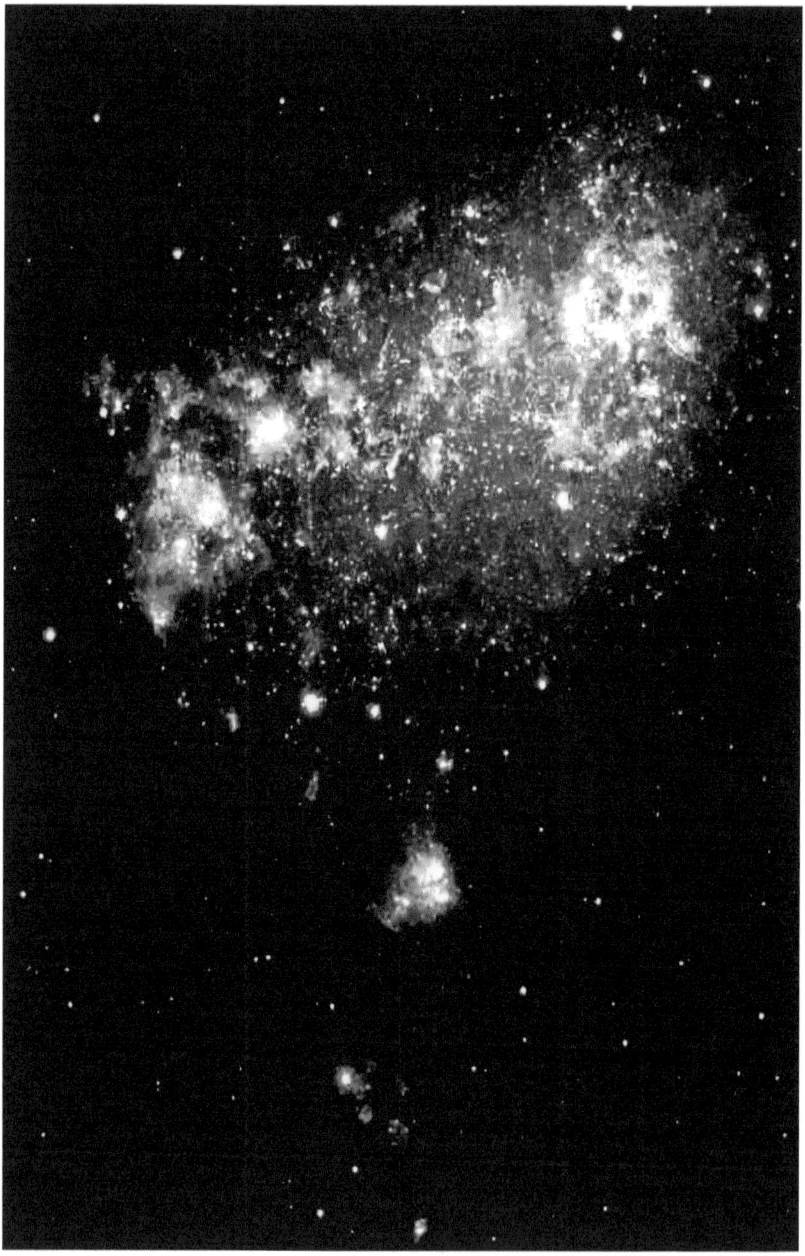

… … rather blue …

even the devil
writhes

enlightened
by the flames
that are the fire
that he is

is it safe
to grasp
a demon's tail

is it
safe
to speak aloud
his story

I would rather
read the book
penned
silent blue
in smoke

I would rather
if he must burn
that he burn
alone

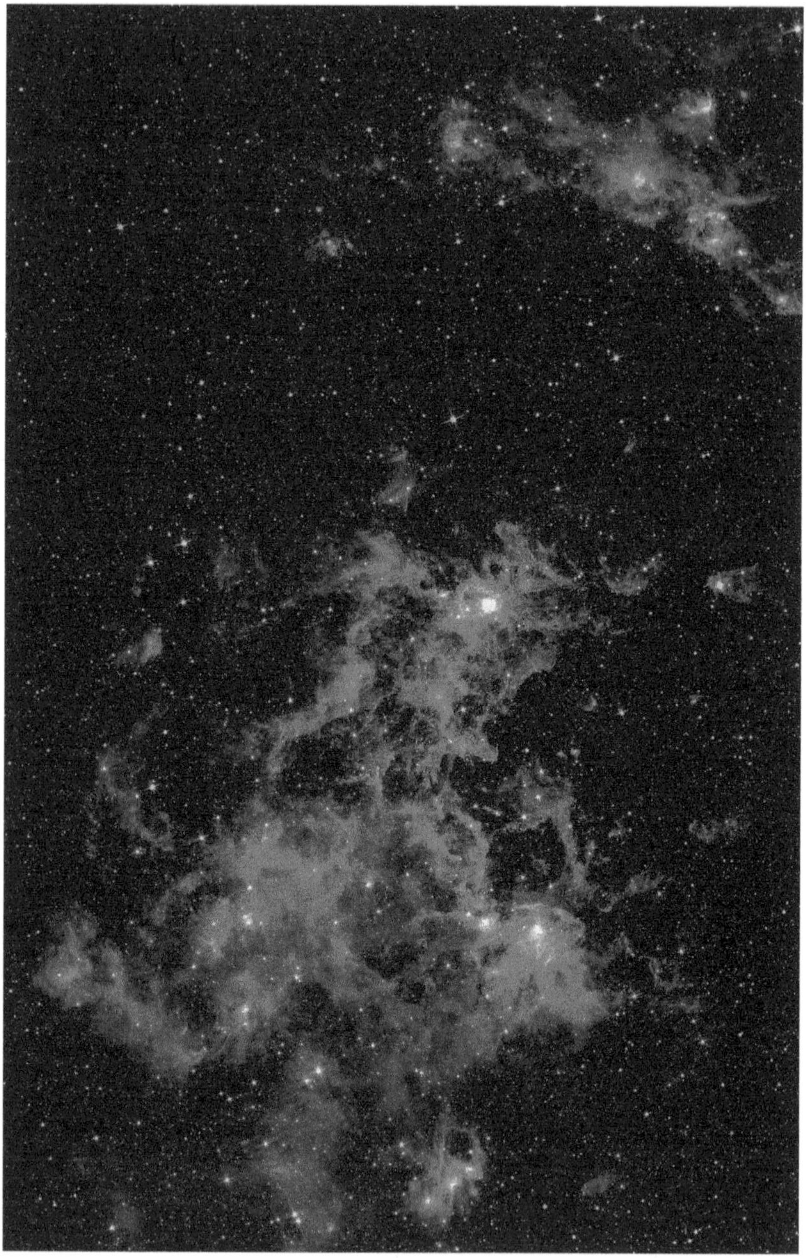

... ... dare ...

who dares
the fire god

who would stand
on his threshold

he waits
he waits

all of time
may pass

what is time
but a moment
of thought

one
idle moment

come
let us dare
together

wept

it frightens him
when he hears the sound
of laughter

he knows
it comes from
within

he is aware
that his situation
is not *humorous*
at all

but sometimes
he also knows
that *he* is the only source
of laughter

ha ha ha ha
HA HA HA
hahaha ha ha haha
ha
ha
ha

he cannot stop
weeping

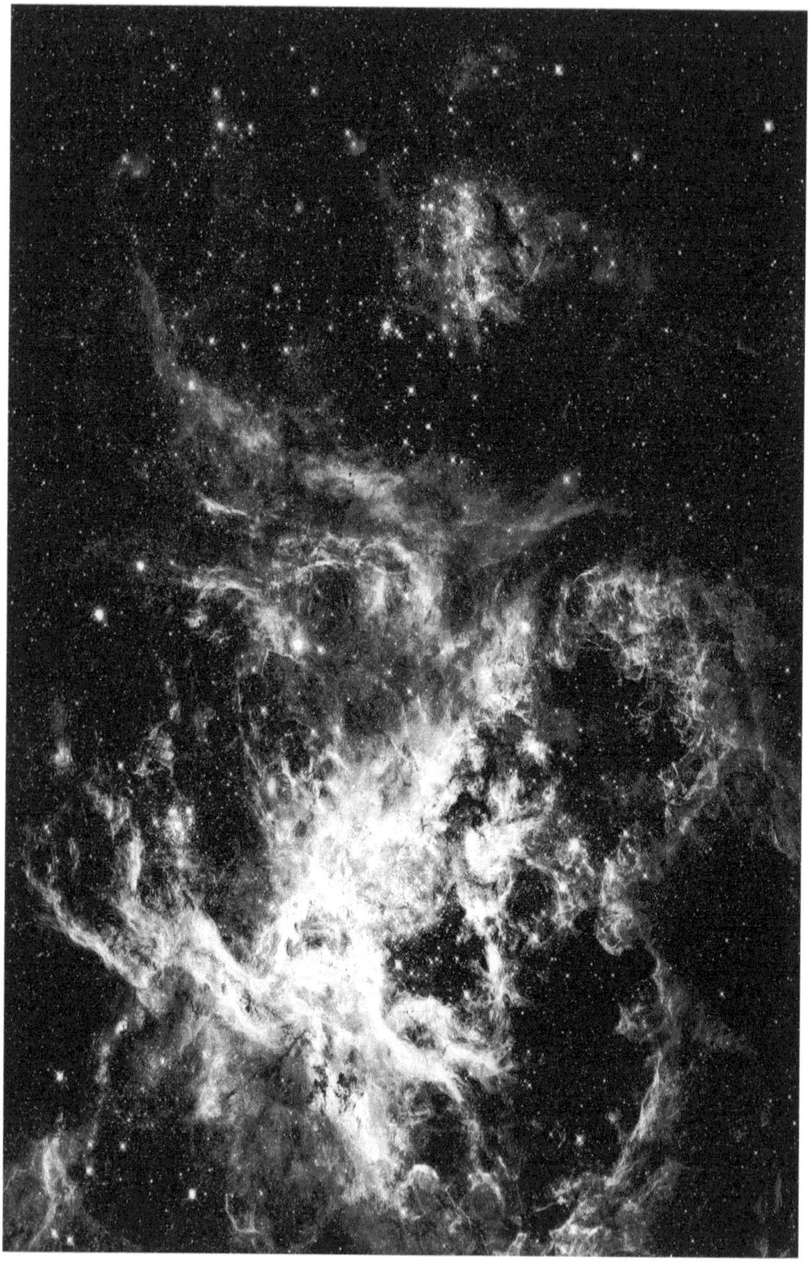

… … the way I find …

I

thread a path
through
the spider's web

I
find a way
through storms

I unravel
the road ahead

I find
but . . .

I never know

... ... coloured the same ...

child
of dreams
the stars shine
to light your night

child
of night

shine
brighter
than they

visions
and images

the opening
of a flower

child of sleep
dream the world
alive

... ... time (to shine . . .)

as deep
as is
night
I will rise

I will
choose
my own right time
to shine

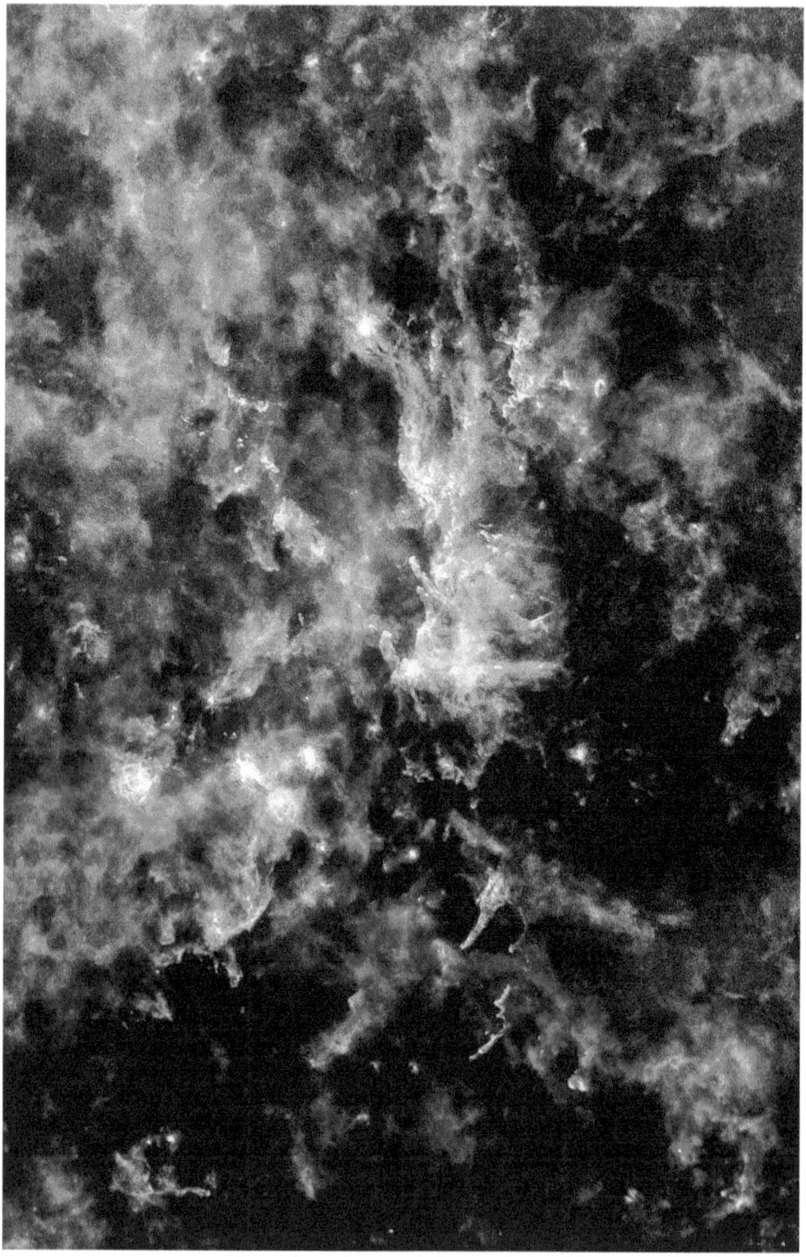

… … of you …

and I am the miner

I fossick
and scrape

dig
where I can
for your jewels

.
.
.

hold them
to the light

scan them
for colour

touch them
to feel for the traces

the hints
and suggestions
that might tell me

these
are of you

knight move

another game
of spoken chess

the ship-machinery
spares him
a tiny portion
of its mind

he has tried to influence
but
it is too busy
thinking

the dark outside
wanders slowly
past the port

.
.
.

a pattern of squares
in three dimensions
on a wall
indicates
a knight move

he is the king
and knows
that every game he plays
he will
lose

his ship
is implacable
in its mate-ing of him
and he is the pawn

who’s place it is
to be sacrificed

to be taken down
in the long game

check

the voice comes
from all around him

it feels like
the only time
he is noticed

check

wherever
he moves

check

whenever
he moves

check

even when he feels
that he cannot move

mate

he is beaten

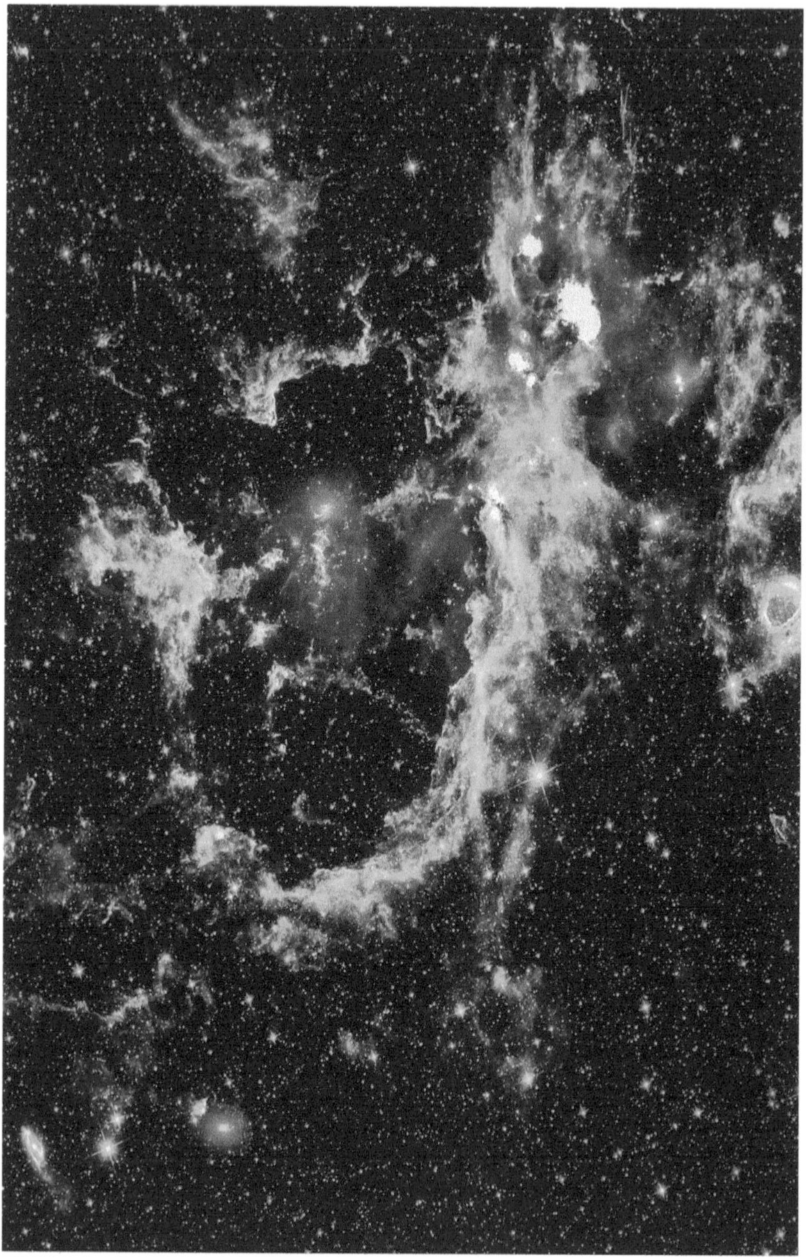

... ... the beating heart ...

a beating heart

my
beating
heart

I carry it slow
I keep it safe

it beats
a deep slow song
for me

wherever
I go

... ... alice and me ...

a white rabbit

a black hole
in space

me

I must be
alice

perhaps
I'm late

or perhaps
this small ship
this large journey
this endless voyage away

is going
to eat me

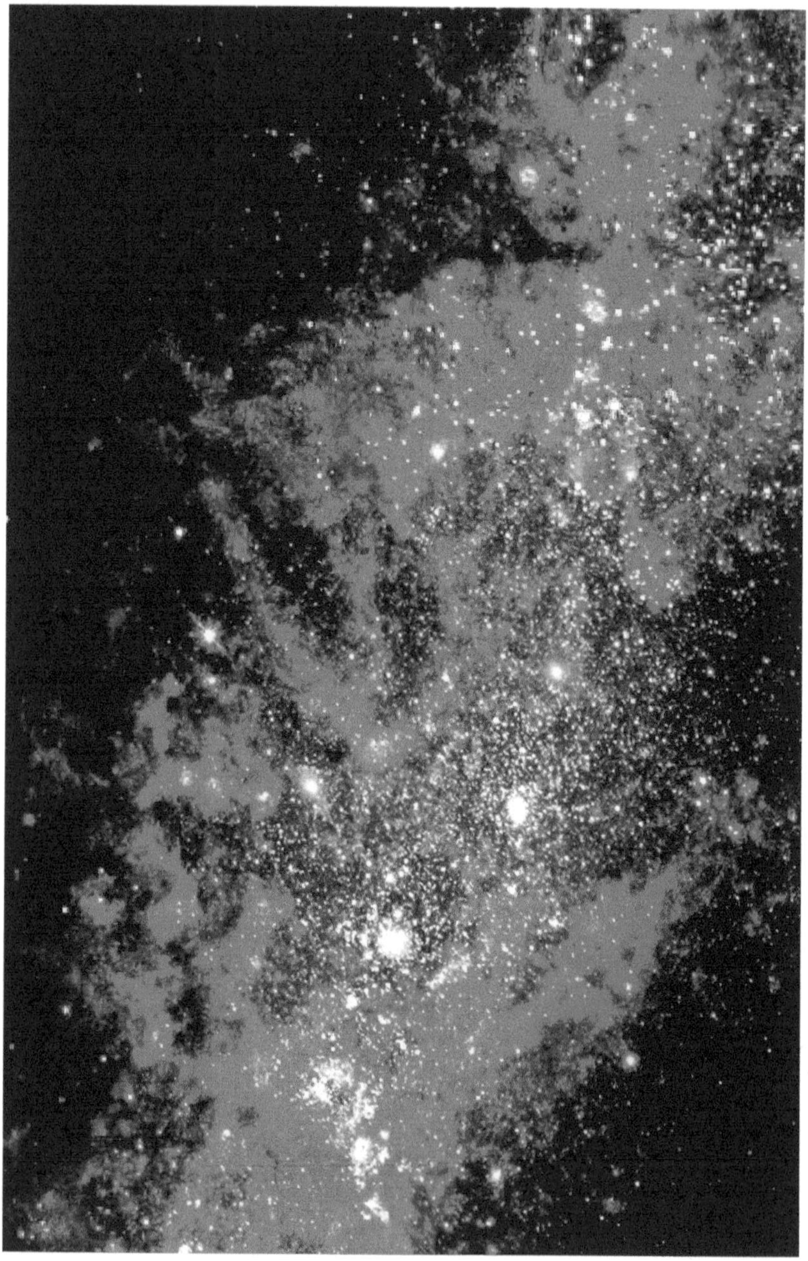

... ... am gone ...

I don't see you
clearly
any more

you seem so
there
while I am
here

sometimes
I fear that I have lost you
in the crowd

sometimes
I'm sure
that you can't see me

I don't stand out
from my background
anymore

once upon a time
I believe
I shone

.
.
.

look this way
I am waving

(waving)

look this way . . .

no
it's too late

I
am gone

… … a kind of christmas …

the mœdƏaƏ
gather
out among the stars

worship
for the new-born
stellar

somewhere
sometime

it must be
a kind
of christmas

self (to self)sometimes

a conversation starts

a voice speaks
from outside the porthole window

it follows him
from glass
to glass
as he wanders

it could be
the ship itself
speaking

it could be god

the darkness

likely
more likely
it is his own mind
thinking
in a two-way thought

the rational
become
much more elusive

but
to talk to another
even in illusion

even in delusion

even
in psychosis
is divine

about nothing
about something
about the lightyears
passed
since the last time

he finds
he speaks his thoughts
aloud
hoping for encounter

he becomes
a version of
the-bitter-soul
when the only sound
he can hear
is himself

... ... my own rose ...

sometimes
a rose will bloom

out of the darkness

right before
my eyes

a flower
will open
in its own garden

sometimes
there are things I know

revelations
only mine

and sometimes
there is no one

no one
to tell them to

I tell myself

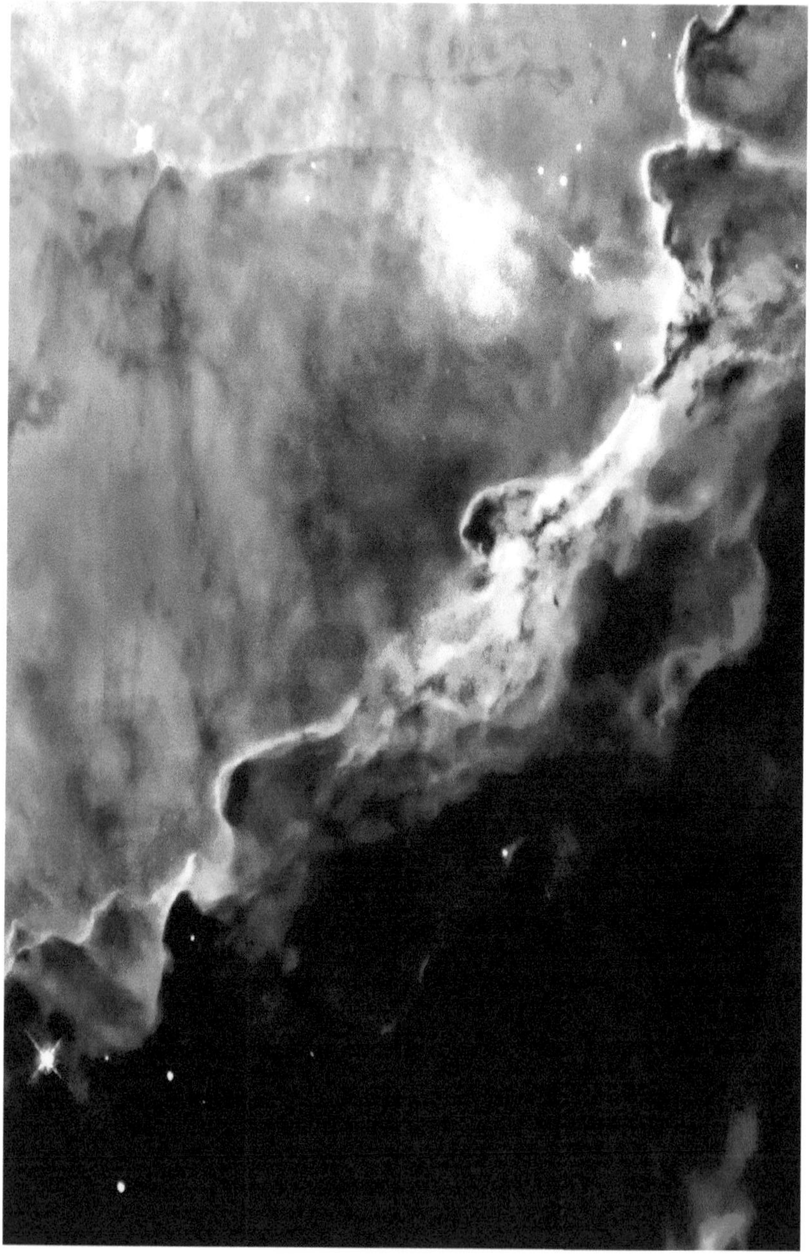

… … shadows (on every star) …

shadows
in the dark
move

I
am sleeping

that does not stop
the creep
through time

sometimes close

sometimes
in my mind

sometimes
I wish
upon each star

on every star
that I leave
behind me

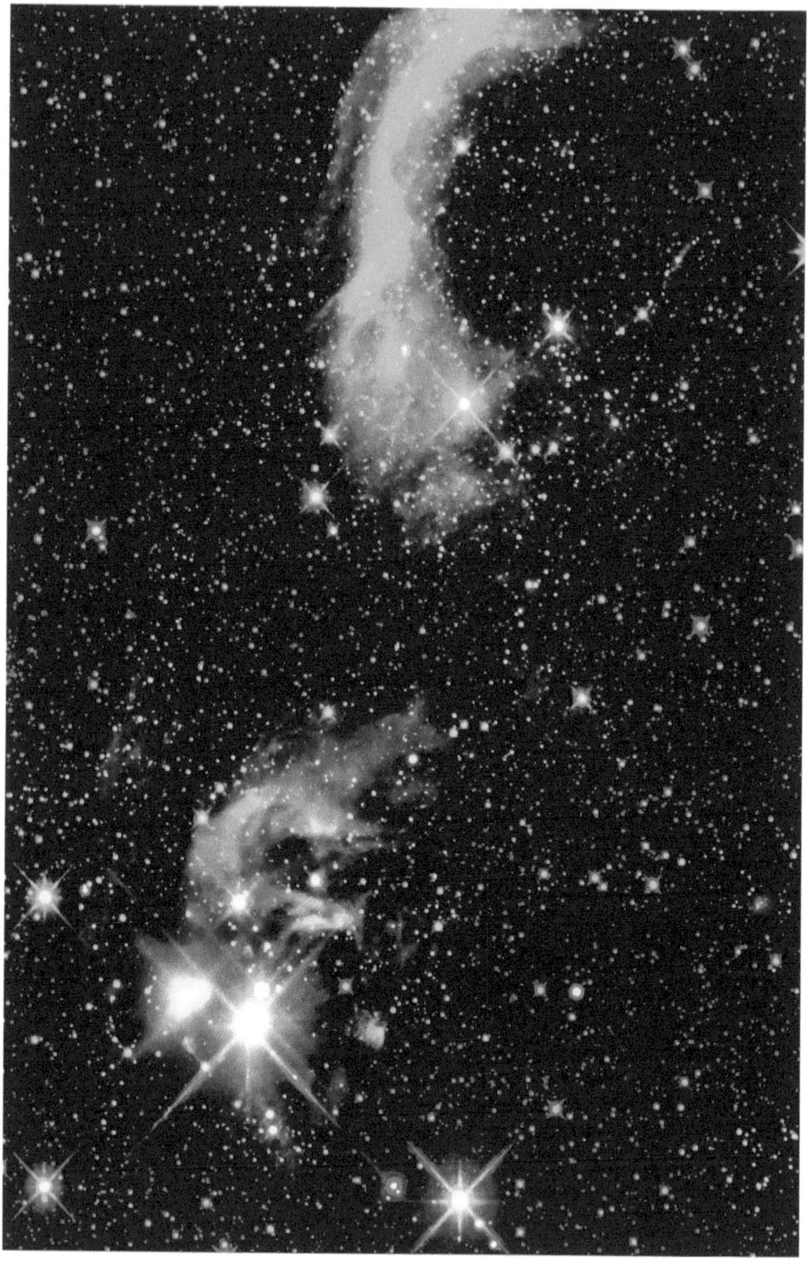

… … I see you close …

what is
alone

who
is alone

is it ever the truth
that there is no
one

I hear a voice

I hear
your voice

as close as
right now

if I look through
the glass
I will see you

I
am not alone
when
I hear your voice
and
almost
I can see you . . .
close

… … *what question* …

stir
the cauldron

watch the steam
writhe

there

deep
in the turmoil
will be
an answer

is it what you want

is it what you
need

is it what you thought
you were
asking

stir
the cauldron

watch the steam

your answer
comes

wild laughter

awake
in darkness

these hours
are set
as his personal night-time

ten hours . . .

twelve

of
only the cosmos
glowing

it doesn't matter

isn't real

it is just a routine
that he has held to
since day one

a pretence
diurnal
to play at being normal

out
through the glass
is a state
of *no-light*

black
is the condition
of *what-there-is*

except for pinpoints
white specks
blue and red

and one yellow
that is
growing

he wonders
what does it
mean

nose
to the porthole
in an attempt
to visually confirm

what does it mean

the sound
of a bristly beard

is it
a made object

does it have
some kind
of purposeful direction

will it make
a course adjustment
to align
with his own
no-direction

will his ship speak
at last
send out a call . . .

a greeting . . .

is this over

almost over

he hears the sound
of his own
wild
laughter

clutches
the console bear

… … even alone …

in this game
we are all
six-sided
random

number small
number large

all
just numbers
the same

tumbling
over the spot

over the six

over
the dice
that keep us in play

even
alone

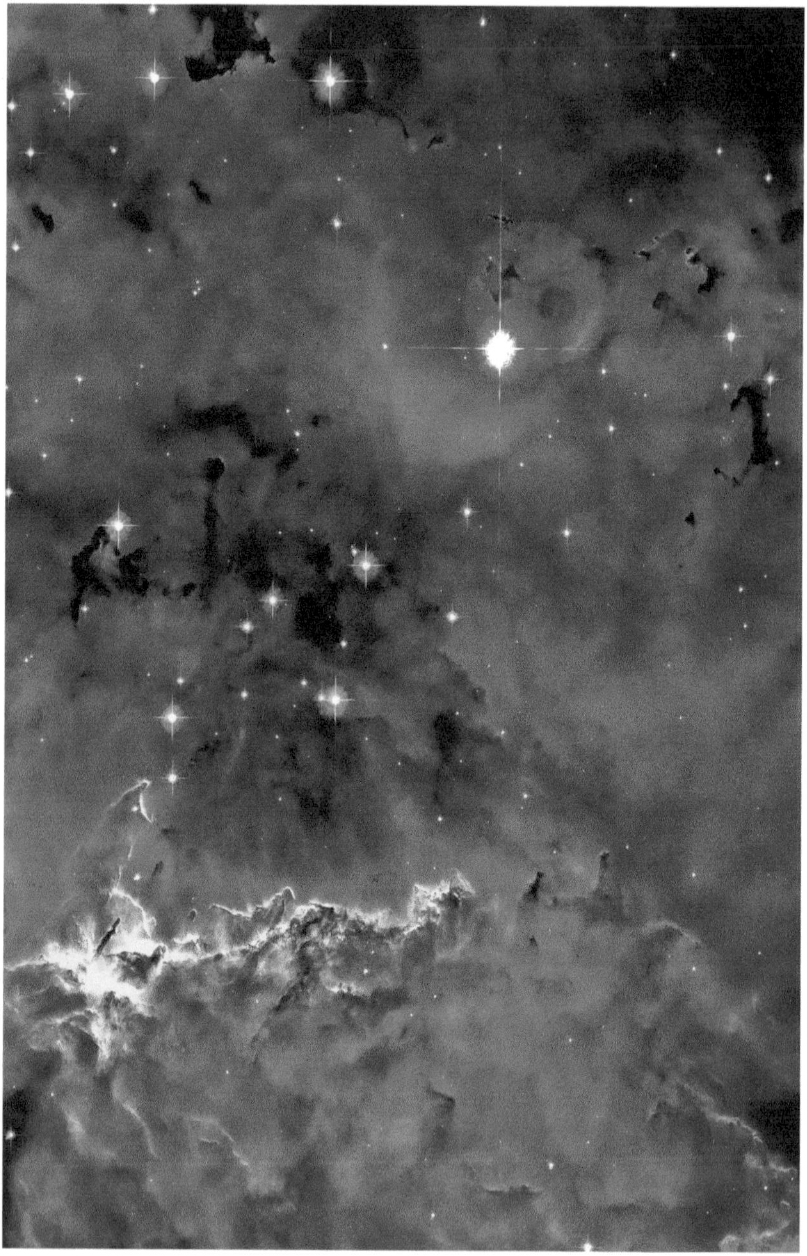

... ... guide ...

a light
will shine
through dust
and darkness

will bright the earth
beneath my feet

a colour signal
of
rising dawn

I take my fear
I hold my breath
I wait

until the light
shines
full upon my face

like every
lost and lonely
I wait

light
to be
my guide

… … only a passing …

one is a star

two is a
cloud

three is a colour
that I
cannot tell you

maybe alive

maybe
just shape

look . . .

look again

is this
brightness
only the light
of a dying
sun

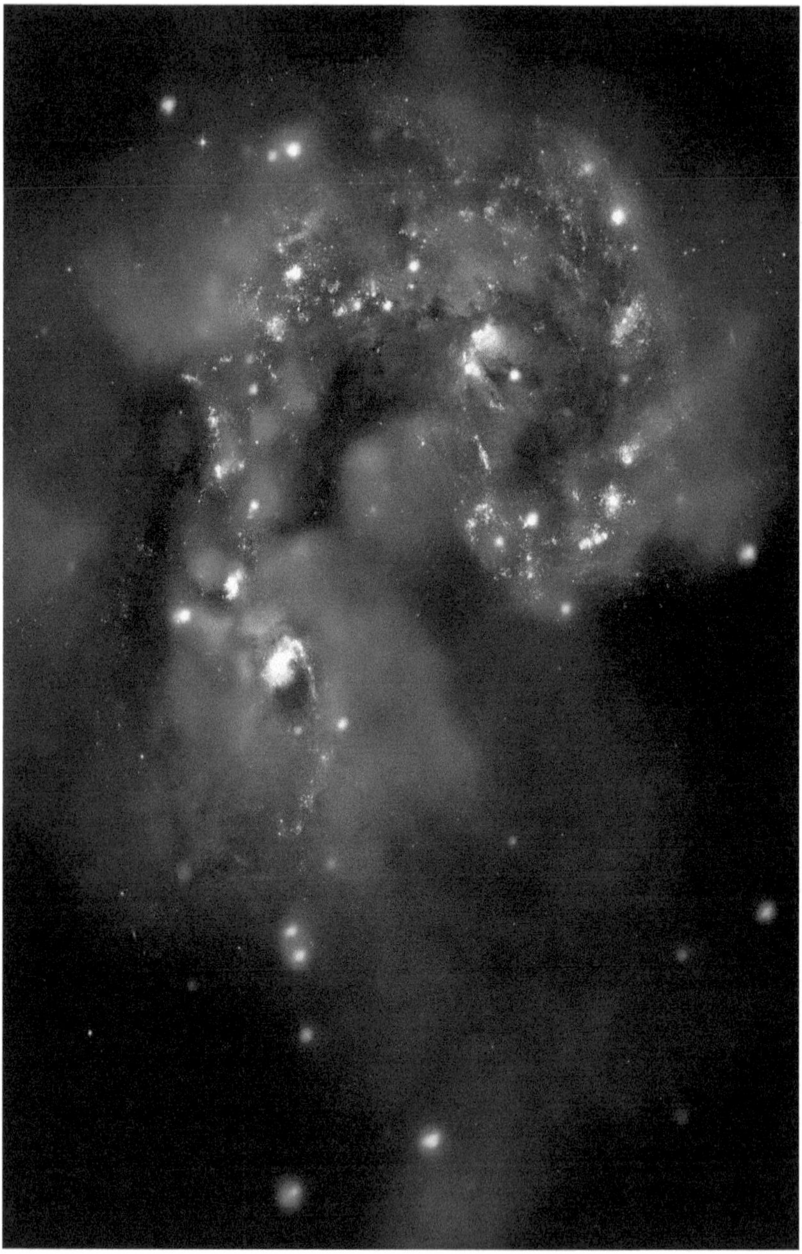

... ... a wonder I wander ...

the question
is

the question
remains

what is my place
here
in the stars

I know the answer

I feel it
close

but when I speak
aloud
it is just
myself

again
fate decrees
that I wonder

as fate decrees
still
I wander

at the end the fire

and at the last
he is
an older man

passenger
through a long
long
lifetime

yet
every journey
has its own end

the only world he had known –
forever young in his mind –
has been buried
long ago
beneath the dust
of light

and is gone

now
he watches
an unblinking eye

he has stared at it
for years
as he still measures
his own life time

yellow
red
and flaring

a destination

there is
a kind of comfort

a thin veneer
that conceals despair

for so long
he thought
his ship
was going to no
where

or that it . . .

that *he*
was going to be saved

but no

he can imagine now
this
so much more certain
ending

the phoenix
in reverse

a cielo-bird
with himself on board
plunging
into fire

and then . . .

should he
believe
in rebirth

recall
the old tales
of a heaven

of a hell

should he chant
out loud
some sutra
or find a set
of worry beads
and begin to count them
down

there will be a conclusion
this time
he is sure

a hot one

there is an end
and his days
have almost passed

here
the finale
will be to dive into the heart
of a star

a very minor supernova
performed
on a uniquely personal scale

the unblinking eye
does not see
him

it does not care

but he –
when he closes his eyes –
he knows

the fire comes
at the end

… … (always) coming home …

in my heart
the world
remains

as true
as yesterday

kissing winds
and wandering clouds

I am the son
always
coming home
at last

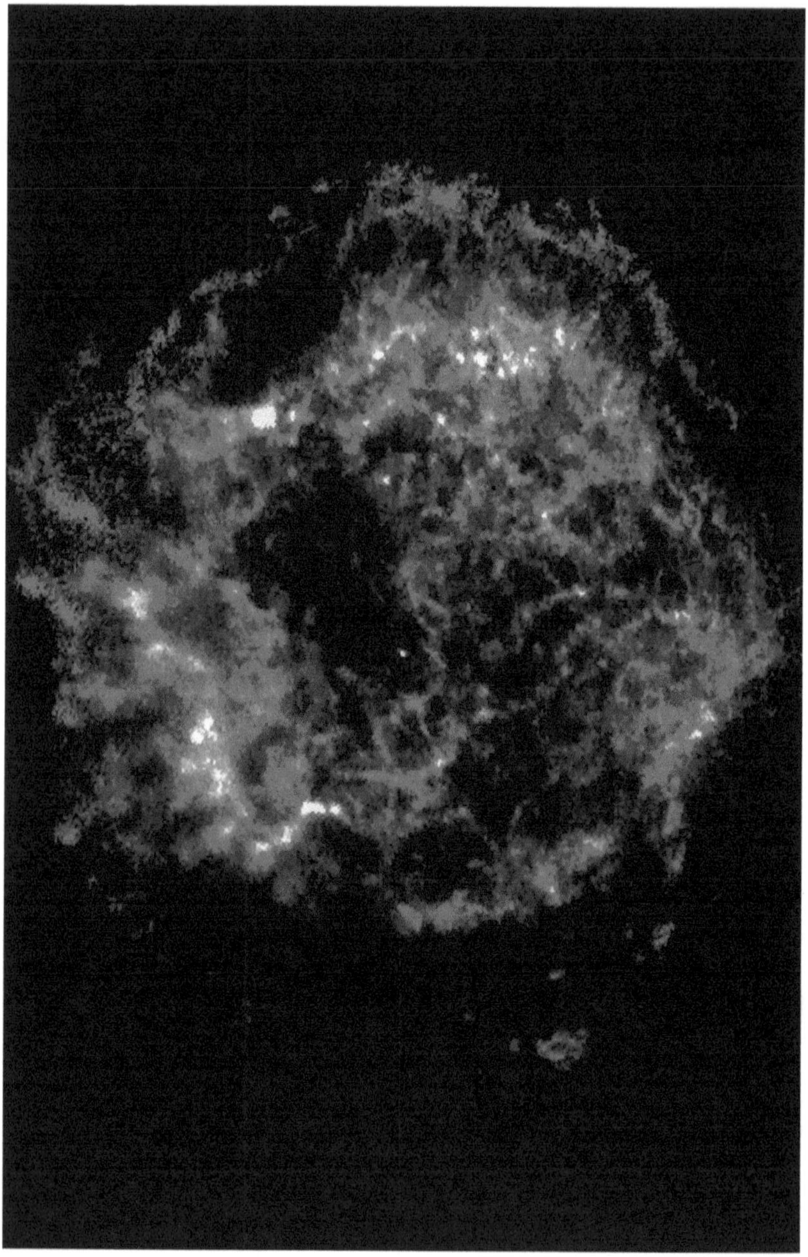

... ... an approaching flame ...

fire
will come

I feel it now

a heat
that flows
from the heart

from
the flame

... ... wheel around ...

the stars wheel

I
go around

like a child
arms wide
and turning

I am a kaleidoscope
at play

dizzy now

I stand
you spin

mesmerise me
into believing
you
might know
the way

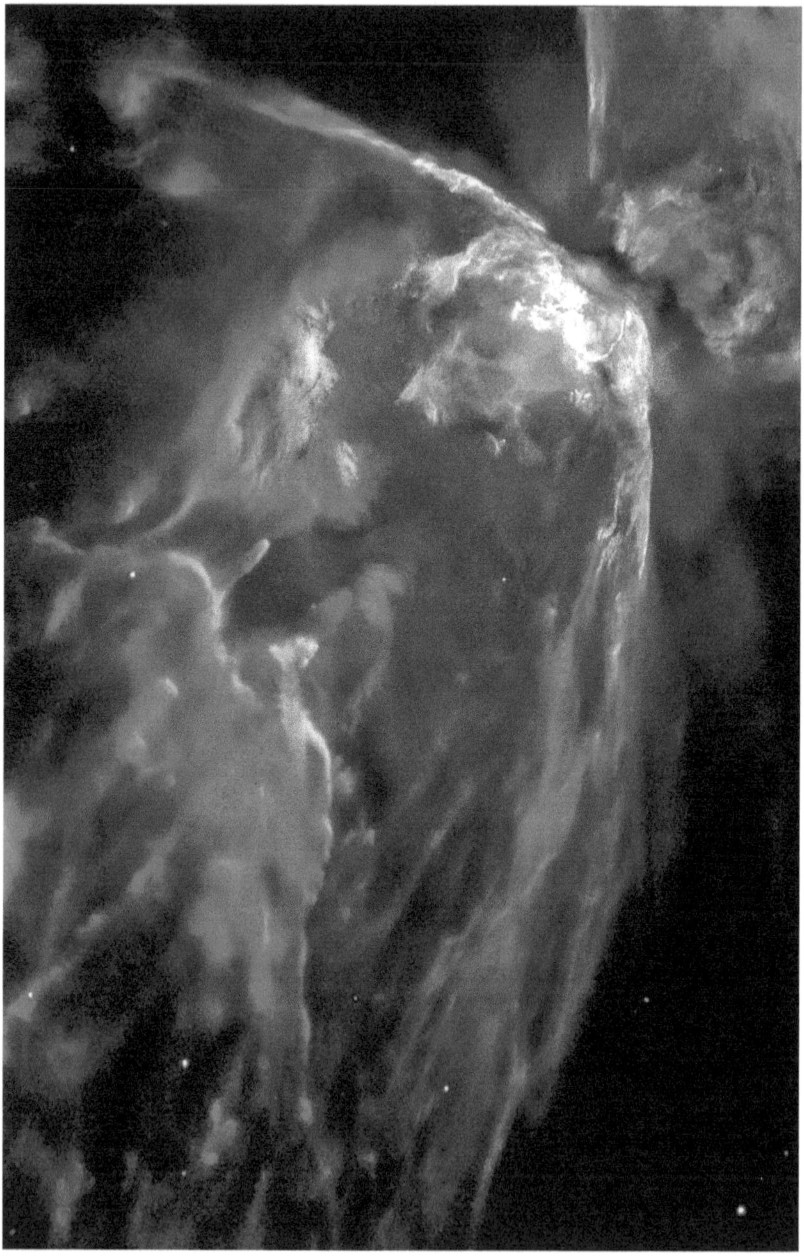

… … leaving (again) …

and somehow
even though
I am going
to

in my mind
my heart
I know

this
is really
leaving

and my journey
already old
is a separation
that I feel

as though new
again

phoenix (a reading)

the all-seeing
never-blinking
does not register
a tremor

it accepts
a tiny bullet
like an offering
that is its due

a supplication
to god

the transition
is completed
and there has been no alteration
in the equilibrium
of the universe

the great eye
does not see
or perhaps
it does not care
that a small *datapac*
is fleeing

back
out
and along the inbound trajectory
that will one day
in another lifetime
embrace old earth
should that place still survive

just as a prodigal
might clutch at the soil
of home

the data
is in the shape
of a bird
on fire

a virtuoso
form

the phoenix
has burned

but the phoenix
may rise again
at the reading
of one
last
poem
encrypted and clutched
within the heart
of a fleeing
datapac

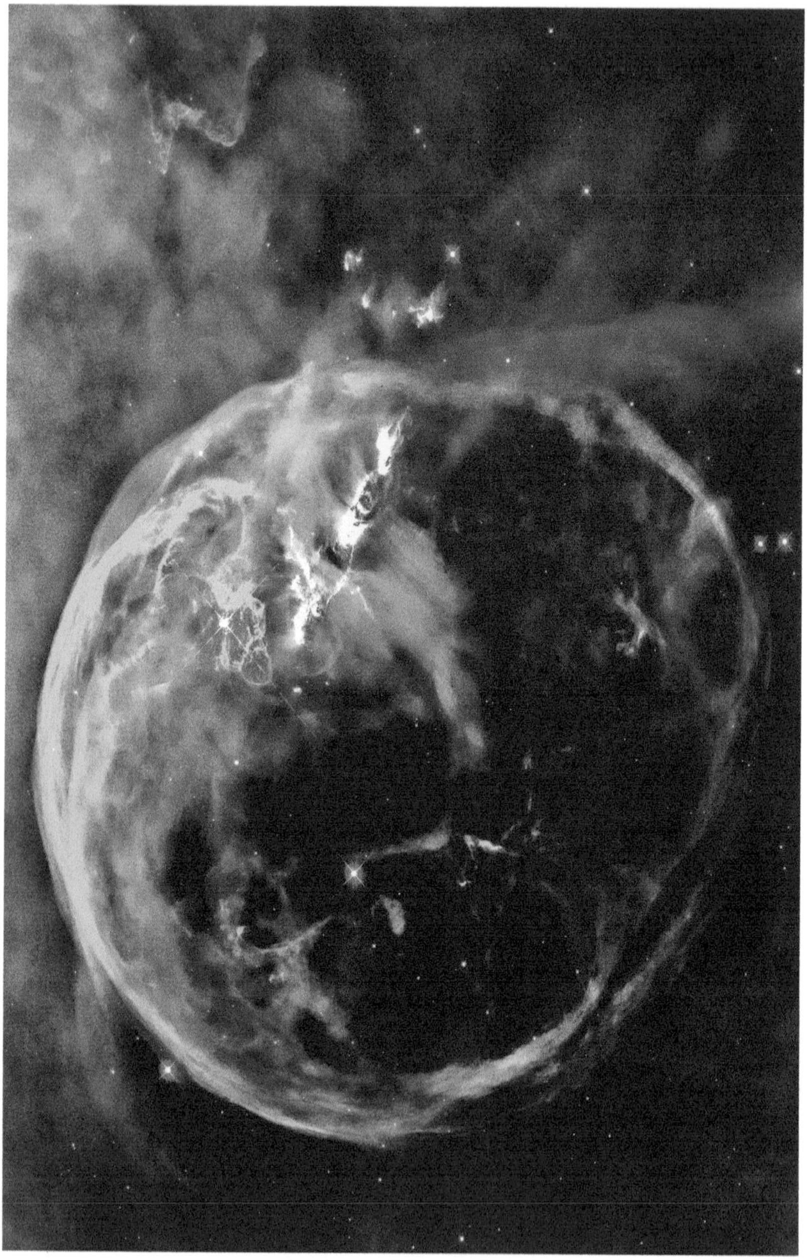

… … in the bubble I saw (an illusion of blue) …

for a moment
I saw . . .

saw
I suppose
what I wished
to see

blue in a bubble

memories
of home

an illusion
drawn on a grander scale
than my own
imagination

but that –
in the end –
is just . . .

the end

a bubble bursts . . .

and then
is gone

and so my dreams
are proven

the end
is waiting

… … too much …

the missing piece . . .

is me
perhaps

maybe a yellow
turned
to white

too heavy for the line

too different
to remain

too alone

an other path

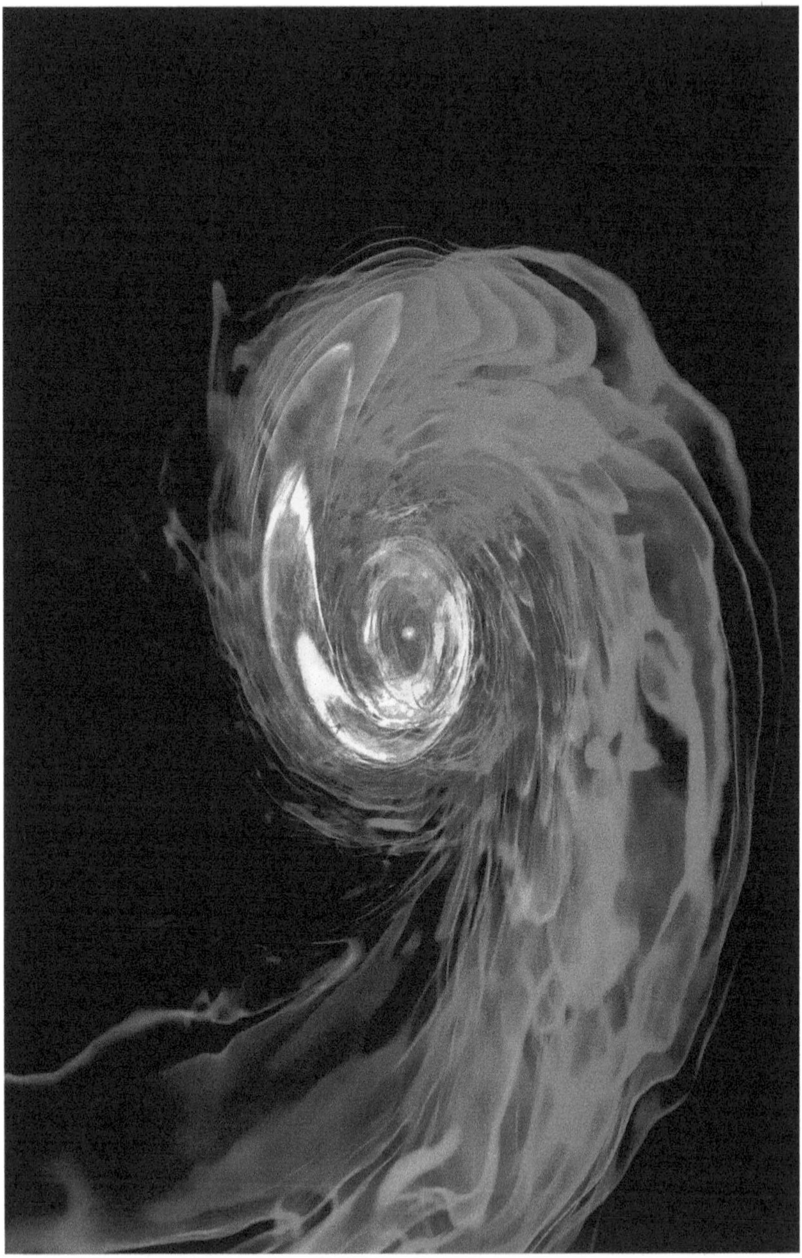

... ... firebird ...

firebird
rise

accept
the soul of me

preen me
into each
of your feathers

firebird
firebird
rise up
to fly me home

I am weary
wandering

firebird

into each feather
place a little
of the heart
of me

let's
you and I
find a way
to go home

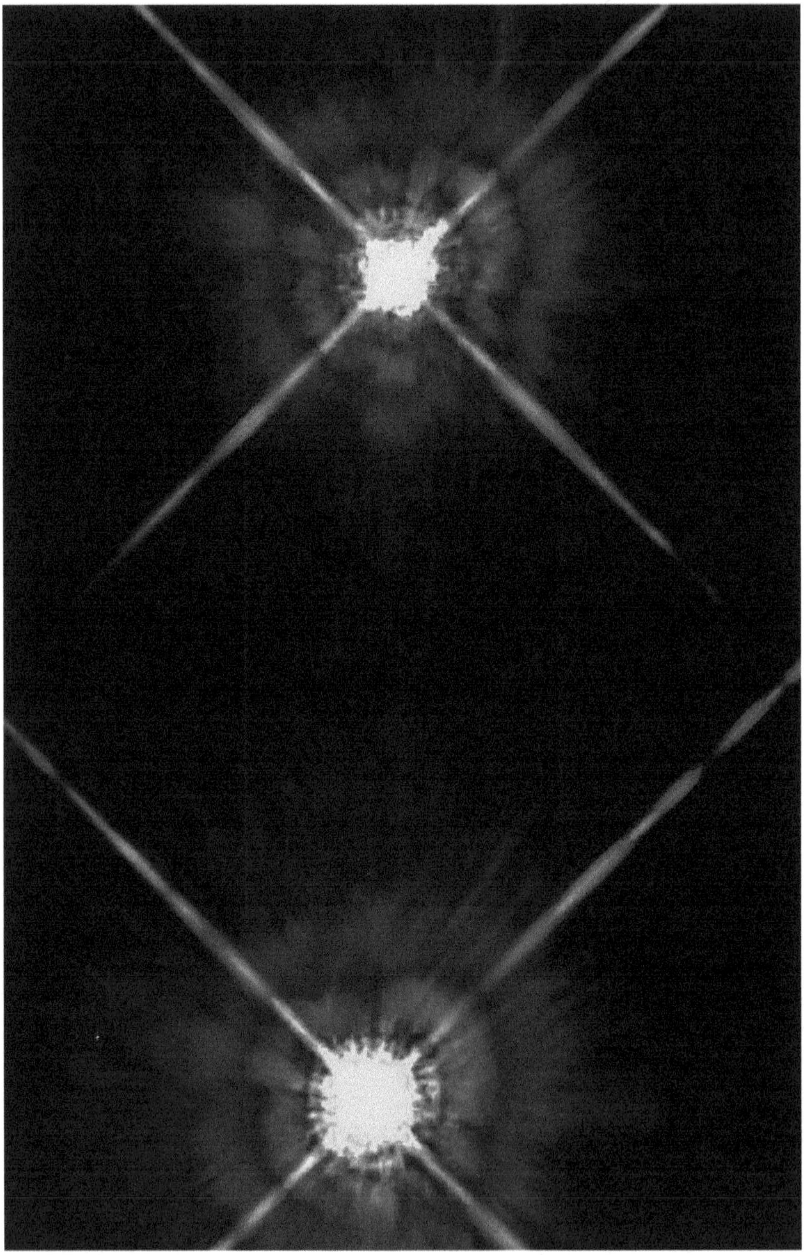

... ... drawn ...

and blind
as I still
must seem

yet
I welcome this journey
towards light

it shines –
my guiding star –
and I wander
slowly

sometimes
too fast

but always
I wander
towards
this brightness

it draws me
on

a song: an epilogue

there is safety
in the habitat

risks are small

choice
is wide

there is room
to run

room to be as free
as an *image-cast*
will allow

children play

adults
perform allotted tasks

no problems

roof
is sky

grass yields
underfoot

pleasant

so
why step out
into the badlands

why breathe
the acrid sharpness
of unfiltered air

why stand
eyes raised
towards the sky

and why
this moment

.
.
.

something new
flies
around the red sun

something old
that brings a taste
of blue

it is a bird

it is a song
it is a message
is a gift
from the far beyond

and here
standing outside *the habitat*
a choir has been
drawn

an assembly of souls
with voices raised
toward vermillion

to sing

… … I become …

don't sing
sad songs for me

I am here
and I am a part
of all of this

now I burn

in my own way
a star

at the end
I become
the fire

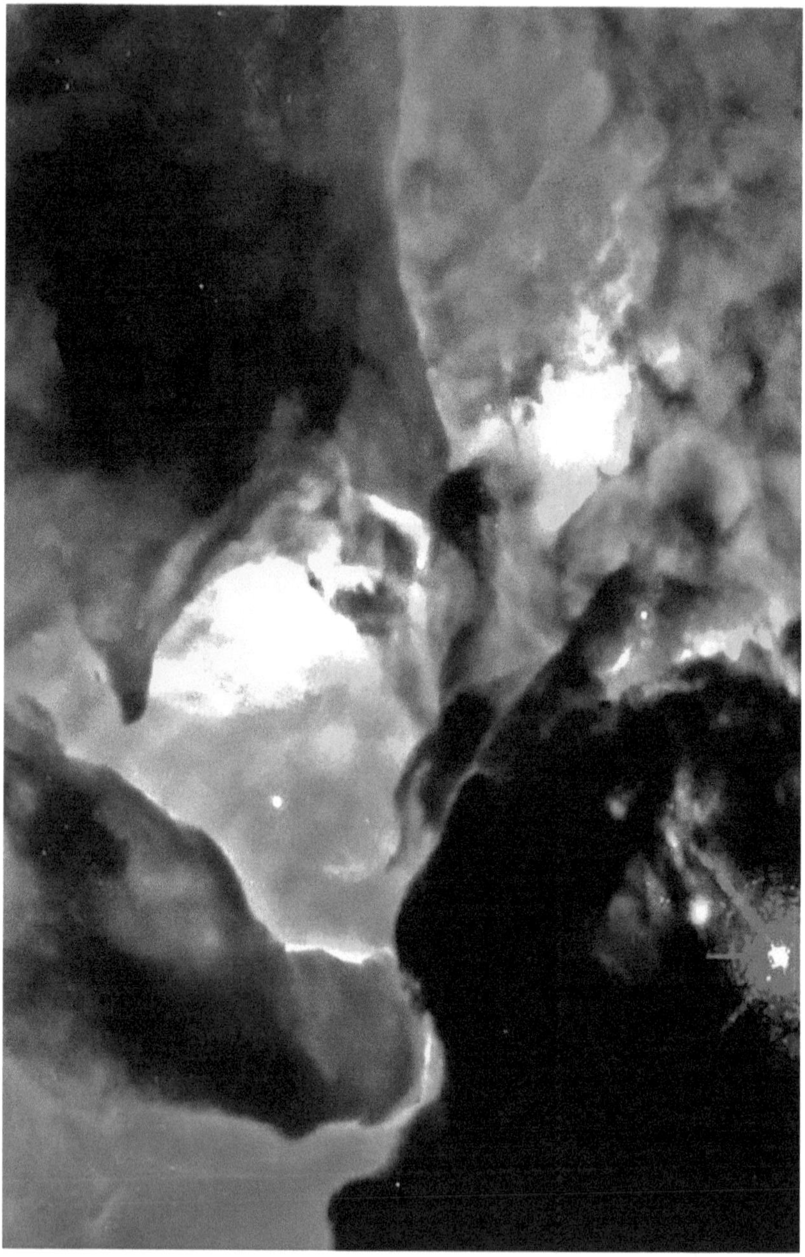

… … where I go …

whatever
I become

wherever
I should stray

in some way
I will take you
with me
where I go

and I do not see
the end

I see
only
my stars

in some way
they will take me
with them
where I go

… … upon the dust …

upon the day
when dust
remains

remember me

your shooting star

I was aimed
straight

and I flew
as true as the universe
allowed

in a memory
no more
than mist
I will search

find my way
perhaps
to home

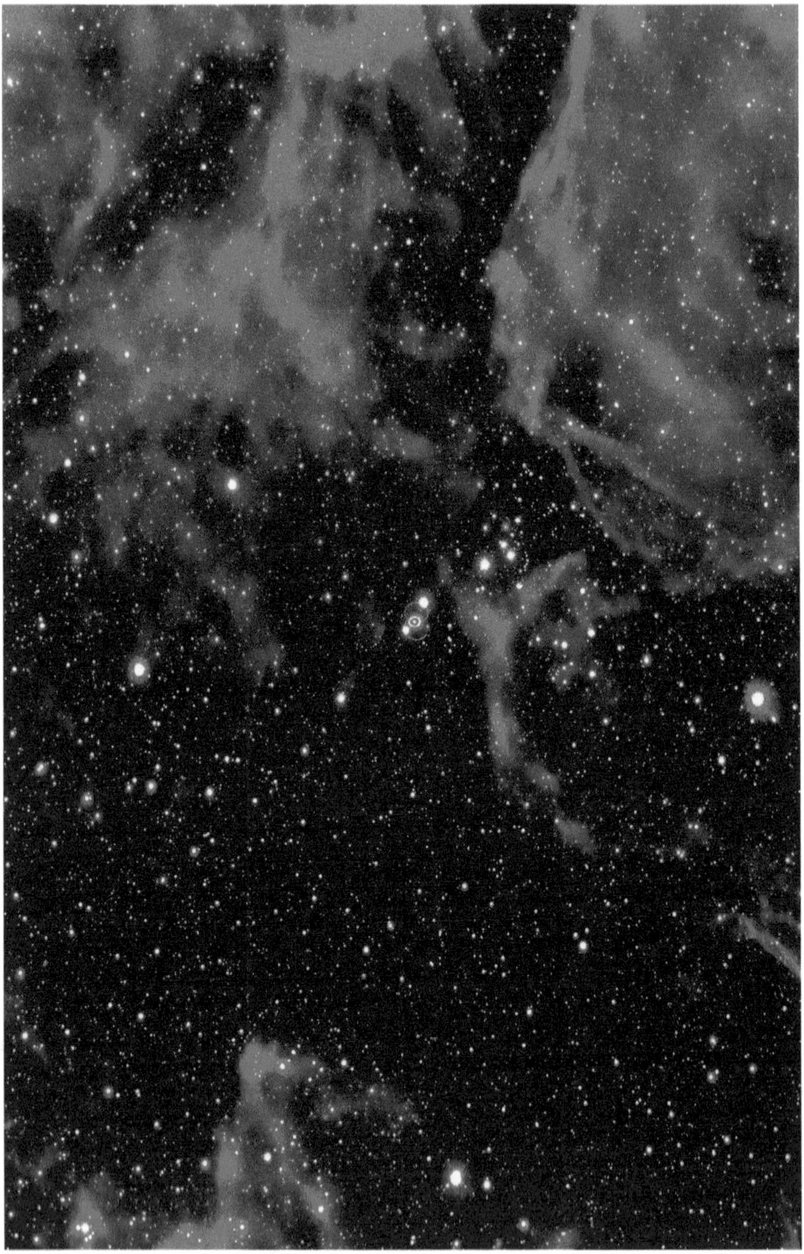

… … (još uvijek zadivljen) under heaven …

sve postoji pod nebom

everything exists
under heaven

sve
što nam dolazi
od tih zvijezda
koji sjaji

everything
that comes to us
from the stars that shine
down upon me

and me . . .

I run toward them

me . . .

I will meet them
where they will

I gaze out
at the soft light

od tih zvijezda

of these stars

i pitam se

and I ask myself

postoji li život
gdje
jedan
od ovih dana
čak ja

is there life
where
one of these days
even I

morat ću
stići

must finally arrive

I look
at the stars . . .

još uvijek ispunjen
sam
s čudenjem

even now I am
filled
with wonder

I gaze

još uvijek
zadivljen

even now
amazed

Image Sources

NASA Image and Video Library

All images used in *The Cielonaut* have been sourced from the NASA Image and Video Library. The author highly recommends this wonderful resource.

Please note: Some of the images may no longer reside at their original NASA locations. A little investigation may be required to access them in the present day.

Image Links

a coming flame: https://images.nasa.gov/details-9905485.html
a kind of christmas: https://images.nasa.gov/details-PIA03096.html
a laugh around: https://images.nasa.gov/details-0700064.html
a wonder I wander: https://images.nasa.gov/details-A%20Galactic%20Spectacle_4862916839_o.html
alice and me: https://images.nasa.gov/details-PIA04200.html
already claimed: https://images.nasa.gov/details-PIA16022.html
always coming home: https://images.nasa.gov/details-GSFC_20171208_Archive_e000496.html
am gone: https://images.nasa.gov/details-0400391.html
beacon, I follow: https://images.nasa.gov/details-KSC-06pd2733.html
by the veil: https://images.nasa.gov/details-GSFC_20171208_Archive_e000933.html
coloured the same: https://images.nasa.gov/details-GSFC_20171208_Archive_e001777.html
dance with the scorpion: https://images.nasa.gov/details-PIA13128.html
dare: https://images.nasa.gov/details-PIA14885.html
drawn: https://images.nasa.gov/details-GSFC_20171208_Archive_e000214.html
drop and run: https://images.nasa.gov/details-GSFC_20171208_Archive_e000671.html
eagle care: https://images.nasa.gov/details-GSFC_20171208_Archive_e000842.html
eternity waiting: https://images.nasa.gov/details-PIA04609.html
even alone: https://images.nasa.gov/details-iss040e006093.html
eye of the night: https://images.nasa.gov/details-PIA16604.html
firebird: https://images.nasa.gov/details-GSFC_20171208_Archive_e001101.html
first: https://images.nasa.gov/details-PIA18014.html
flows green my heart: https://images.nasa.gov/details-PIA09411
for orion: https://images.nasa.gov/details-PIA13448.html
from you: https://images.nasa.gov/details-7461902.html
go by: https://images.nasa.gov/details-PIA04934.html
good night: https://images.nasa.gov/details-GSFC_20171208_Archive_e001513.html
guide: https://images.nasa.gov/details-GSFC_20171208_Archive_e002063.html
I become: https://images.nasa.gov/details-GSFC_20171208_Archive_e001061.html
I come: https://images.nasa.gov/details-iss036e006073.html
I see you close: https://images.nasa.gov/details-PIA13064.html
in the bubble I saw: https://images.nasa.gov/details-GSFC_20171208_Archive_e000383.html
leaving again: https://images.nasa.gov/details-GSFC_20171208_Archive_e002086.html
my love sees: https://images.nasa.gov/details-PIA17553.html
my own rose: https://images.nasa.gov/details-PIA05266
ochre: https://images.nasa.gov/details-PIA13005.html
of you: https://images.nasa.gov/details-PIA13500.html

oh heart: https://images.nasa.gov/details-a-hubble-cosmic-couple_20140593234_o.htm
on: https://images.nasa.gov/details-iss036e005813
one more turn around: https://images.nasa.gov/details-behemoth-black-hole-found-in-an-unlikely-place_26209716511_o.html
only a passing: https://images.nasa.gov/details-PIA03244.html
rather blue: https://photojournal.jpl.nasa.gov/jpegMod/PIA12485_modest.jpg
rock the table: https://images.nasa.gov/details-GSFC_20171208_Archive_e000193.htm
search for blue: https://images.nasa.gov/details-0302062.html
shadows on every star: https://images.nasa.gov/details-0302063.html
shine: https://images.nasa.gov/details-PIA10957.html
sing (a birthday song): https://images.nasa.gov/details-PIA13100.html
swim: https://images.nasa.gov/details-GSFC_20171208_Archive_e000637.html
the beating heart: https://images.nasa.gov/details-PIA13112
the way I find: https://images.nasa.gov/details-GSFC_20171208_Archive_e001777.html
time to shine: https://images.nasa.gov/details-PIA16008.html
too much: https://images.nasa.gov/details-PIA19645.html
(još uvijek zadivljen) under heaven : https://images.nasa.gov/details-GSFC_20171208_Archive_e000102.html
upon the dust: https://images.nasa.gov/details-PIA14871.html
what else: https://images.nasa.gov/details-GSFC_20171208_Archive_e000161.html
what might: https://images.nasa.gov/details-GSFC_20171208_Archive_e002064.html
what question: https://images.nasa.gov/details-PIA15254.html
what she will see: https://images.nasa.gov/details-GSFC_20171208_Archive_e001540.html
wheel around: https://images.nasa.gov/details-PIA11999.html
where I go: https://images.nasa.gov/details-9700431.html
young stars: https://images.nasa.gov/details-PIA09411

Author Information

About the Author

Frank Prem has been a storytelling poet since his teenage years. He has been a psychiatric nurse through all of his professional career, which now exceeds forty years.

He has been published in magazines, online zines, and anthologies in Australia, and in a number of other countries, and has both performed and recorded his work as spoken word.

He lives with his wife in the beautiful township of Beechworth in North East Victoria, Australia.

Connect with Frank

As the author, I hope you enjoyed this volume of poetry collection. I think that mine is a unique style of writing that can appeal well beyond a 'pure poetry' readership.

If you enjoyed it, I'd like to ask you to do two small things for me.

First leave a short review of this book with your preferred online retailer by visiting White Whale Universal link and following it to your preferred online retailer leaving a customer review of the book.

Online reviews provide social proof to readers and are critical to Indie authors such as myself.

The second thing is, please pop over to my author page www.FrankPrem.com, and subscribe to receive my occasional Newsletter.

From time to time I'll let you know what is happening with myself and my writing, as well as keeping you informed of any giveaways I may be planning.

You can also find me on Facebook, Twitter, Instagram and YouTube.

Other Publications

Free Verse Poetry

Small Town Kid (2018)

Devil In The Wind (2019)

The New Asylum (2019)

Herja, Devastation - With Cage Dunn (2019)

Walk Away Silver Heart (2020)

A Kiss for the Worthy (2020)

Rescue and Redemption (2020)

Pebbles to Poems (2020)

The Garden Black (2022)

A Specialist at The Recycled Heart (2022)

Ida: Searching for The Jazz Baby (2023)

From Volyn to Kherson (2023)

Alive Is What You Feel (2023)

White Whale (2024)

Picture Poetry/Spoken Image

Voices (In The Trash) (2020)

The Beechworth Bakery Bears (2021)

Sheep On The Somme (2021)

Waiting For Frank-Bear (2021)

A Lake Sambell Walk (2021)

A Few Places Near Home (2023)

What Readers Say

Small Town Kid

A modern-day minstrel

Small-Town Kid is a wonderful collection

—S. T. (Australia)

A poet's walk through his childhood in a small Australian town.

—J. L. (USA)

Devil In The Wind

Instantly grips you by the throat in his step-by-step story of survival.

Bravo!

—K. K. (USA)

Outstanding!

—B. T. (Australia)

The New Asylum

Words can't do justice to the emotional journey I travelled in (reading this collection).

__C. D. (Australia)

If I had to pick one book over the past year that has truly resonated with me, this would be it.

__K. B. (USA)

Walk Away Silver Heart

Has an extraordinary way with words and his poems invoke great passion and emotion in the reader.

—R C (United States)

As Memorable as My Favourite Music

—M D (United States)

A Kiss For The Worthy

A Celebration of Life Written in Thoughtful Bursts of Poetic Expression

—C M C (United States)

With every verse, I found myself reflecting about myself, my life, and the world.

—K

Rescue and Redemption

The passion of love in its many forms explored by one for another.

—J L (United States)

I've enjoyed every word, every breath. Every moment within the life of these stories.

—C D (Australia)

Sheep On The Somme

Museums and archivists take note--sell this in your gift shops, preserve it in your archives. Professors, teachers--share with your students.

—A R C (United States)

(This) book is a beautiful and graphic tribute to all those brave men and women who gave their lives for their countries between 1914 and 1918.

—R C (South Africa)

Ida: Searching for The Jazz Baby

I found myself deeply moved by the presentation of Ida's elusive, illusionary life.

—E G (United States)

He gives her a depth and vulnerability that the press didn't.

— A C (United Kingdom

The Garden Black

Prem creates verse that illuminates our world, its experiences and history. —S C (United Kingdom)

Prem's poetry reminds that life is fragile and fleeting ... both harsh and beautiful.

—D G K (United States)

Herja, Devastation

Simply written, powerfully felt. __C. (Australia)

As a combination of poetry, prose, and wonderfully ominous illustrations, I found Herja, Devastation refreshingly original. Highly recommended!

—G. B. (Australia)

Bravo! Outstanding!

—B. T. (Australia)

Index of Poems

Symbols

… … a kind of christmas … 117
… … a laugh around … 71
… … alice and me … 113
… … already claimed … 79
… … (always) coming home … 147
… … am gone … 115
… … an approaching flame … 149
… … a wonder I wander … 141
… … beacon, I follow … 11
… … by the veil … 27
… … coloured the same … 101
… … dance with the scorpion … 47
… … dare … 95
… … drawn … 165
… … drop and run … 37
… … eagle care … 73
… … eternity waiting … 23
… … even alone … 135
… … eye of the night … 69
… … firebird … 163
… … first … 59
… … flows green my heart … 45
… … for orion … 29
… … from you to me … 57
… … go by … 51
… … good night … 25
… … guide … 137
… … I become … 171
… … I come … 13
… … in the bubble I saw (an illusion of blue) … 159
… … I see you close … 127
… … (još uvijek zadivljen) under heaven … 177
… … leaving (again) … 153
… … my love sees … 91
… … my own rose … 123
… … ochre … 33
… … of you … 105
… … oh heart … 61
… … on … 77
… … one more turn (around) … 55
… … only a passing … 139
… … rather blue … 93
… … rock the table … 89

… … search for blue … 49
… … shadows (on every star) … 125
… … shine … 15
… … sing (a birthday song) … 83
… … swim … 35
… … the beating heart … 111
… … the way I find … 99
… … time (to shine . . .) 103
… … too much … 161
… … upon the dust … 175
… … what else … 67
… … what might … 81
… … what question … 129
… … what she will see … 17
… … wheel around … 151
… … where I go … 173
… … young stars … 39

A

a kind of christmas 117
a little lost 19
a song: an epilogue 167
at the end the fire 143

D

data to the distance 31

E

ever named ever written 63

G

gravity 53

I

in prison for the term of no when 41

K

knight move 107

P

phoenix (a reading) 155
prelude: astro-bear 7

S

self (to self)sometimes 119

T

the sound 75
to catch a star 85

W

wept 97
wild laughter 131

www.FrankPrem.com

Milton Keynes UK
Ingram Content Group UK Ltd.
UKHW052322130524
442620UK00007B/113

9 781925 963557